COLONIAL CLASSICS YOU CAN BUILD TODAY

Colonial Classics You Can Build Today

Plans and drawings for 80 authentic projects, all exact replicas of Early American antiques

John A. Nelson

Stackpole Books

Copyright © 1986 by Stackpole Books

Published by
STACKPOLE BOOKS
Cameron and Kelker Streets
P.O. Box 1831
Harrisburg, PA 17105

All rights reserved, including the right to reproduce this book or portions thereof in any form or by any means, electronic or mechanical, including photocopying, recording, or by any information storage and retrieval system, without permission in writing from the publisher. All inquiries should be addressed to Stackpole Books, Cameron and Kelker Streets, P.O. Box 1831, Harrisburg, Pennsylvania 17105.

Printed in the U.S.A.

Library of Congress Cataloging-in-Publication Data

Nelson, John A., 1935–
   Colonial classics you can build today.

   Includes index.
   1. Furniture making—Amateurs' manuals. 2. Furniture, Early American. I. Title.
TT195.N446   1986   749.214   85-26171
ISBN 0-8117-2025-X

To Frank Barnett of Wakefield, Rhode Island, who has always encouraged and supported my efforts throughout my life. He has, through his knowledge of both wood and antiques, unknowingly helped me write this book. Thank you, Frank.

Contents

Acknowledgments	xi
Preface	xiii
Introduction	xv

Part I
How to Build Colonial Furniture

Origin of Colonial Furniture	2
Wood	2
What Is an Antique	2
Where to Find Antiques	2
Essentials of Design	3
Basic Methods Used to Construct Colonial Furniture	5
Joints	6
Chamfered Bevel Edge	17
Moldings	17
Saw-made Moldings	23
Cove Cuts	23
Drawer Construction	25
Drawer Supports	29
Table Tops	29
To Enlarge a Pattern	32
Transferring the Pattern to the Wood	32
Colonial Hardware	34
Screws	34
Nails	34

Brasses	43
Hinge Sizes and Kinds	50
Patina	51
Finishing Your Project	51
Paint	51
To Apply Paint	51
Wash Coat	52
To Apply Stain	53

Part II
Antique Shelf or Counter Projects

Mortar and Pestles	56
Candle Boxes	59
Utility Boxes	68
Knife Boxes	71
Candle Holder	73
Desk Boxes	75
Blueberry Scoops	81

Part III
Antique Wall Projects

Pipe and Tobacco Boxes	85
Wall Boxes	91
Hanging Shelves	95
Spoon Racks	121
Mirrors	127
Wall Cupboards	129
Apothecary Chests	133
Coffin Clock	135

Part IV
Antique Floor Projects

Stools and Benches	140
Slant-Lid Podium	146
Saw Horse	148
Bucket Bench	151
Dry Sink	153
Dough Box	159
Miniature Cupboard	161

Grain Bin	164
Tables	166
Chairs	180
Chests	185
Lift-Top Commode	197
Wash Stand	199
Formal Pieces	201
Pewter Hutches	205
Beds	211
Cupboards	213
Tall Case Clocks	219

Part V

Appendix

Antique Hardware and Accessories Suppliers	232
Paint	232
Milk Paint	232
Stains/Tung Oil	232
Old-Fashioned Nails/Brass Screws	232
Brasses	232
Veneering	233
General Catalogs	233
Clock Supplies	233
Stenciling Supplies	233
Related Publications and Organizations	234
Museums Where Antique Furniture Can Be Found and Studied	234

The warmth of furniture from the past.
Credit: *Country Antiques*, Fred and Jo Ann Cadarette, Pittsfield, NH.

Acknowledgments

Special appreciation and thanks go to my wife, Joyce, for making sense of my scribbling and poor English and typing it into something that I hope is sensible. Thanks also to my very good friend Jerry Ernce, who first got me interested in woodworking and who gave me the confidence to try it, and to Mr. and Mrs. Derald Radtke, Mr. and Mrs. Joe Brennan, and the many antique dealers and flea market merchants who allowed me to measure and photograph many unique objects in their shops throughout New England. Special gratitude to John Curtis and Henry Peach and to the other fine people of Old Sturbridge Village, Sturbridge, Massachusetts.

Fenno kitchen at Old Sturbridge Village.
Credit: Old Sturbridge Village. Photo by Henry E. Peach.

Preface

This book has been written for two purposes. First, as a woodworkers' guide to reproducing authentic copies of early country and primitive furniture. The second purpose is to keep a record of these wonderful one-of-a-kind objects, lest they be lost forever.

These objects were homespun. They were made by individuals for individuals and reflect the directness and independent spirit of those early craftsmen. These early projects fulfilled a real need once upon a time—this same need can be met today.

This book will provide you with a way to acquire a collection of Early American furniture at a reasonable cost and with a priceless bonus: the satisfaction of making future family heirlooms.

The author sincerely hopes you will enjoy making and living with these projects. Any comments and criticisms from the users of this text are most welcome.

Fitch House, West Parlor at Old Sturbridge Village.
Credit: Old Sturbridge Village. Photo by Henry E. Peach.

Introduction

Furniture of today does not truly capture feelings of warmth and well-being as does furniture from the past. The style of yesteryear's furniture is part of our heritage and our history. The value of antiques as conversation pieces, as works of superior craftsmanship, and as part of the historical record of a society is widely recognized, but their growing scarcity and skyrocketing prices have denied many people the pleasure of decorating their homes with these interesting, attractive, one-of-a-kind pieces.

In years past, these articles were all made by hand, using rather primitive tools by the standards of today. The pieces in this book offer both the amateur with limited equipment and the professional with a full woodworking shop an opportunity to acquire their own collection of Early American furniture.

This book does not attempt to give instructions for making any of these projects; it is offered only as a guide to copying our forefathers' furniture.

Each piece is illustrated by a line drawing of the finished project and a two- or three-view dimensioned drawing giving general, overall sizes. Most projects use basic wood joinery as illustrated in the first part of this book; others, more complicated, will need some thought to learn exactly how they were made. Carefully study each drawing and be sure you understand how you will be putting the project together before starting any actual work. Every attempt has been made to check and verify each dimension and the accuracy of all information, but it is a good idea to reverify each as you proceed on the project.

Remember, the projects in this book are copies of antiques; they will *not* look authentic if they have a shiny, brand-new appearance. In all cases, they will look much more like real antiques if they are distressed slightly. There are many ways to do this, from hitting the project with a chain to shooting it with a shotgun! Some fanatics even bury their projects in a swamp for six months. This is a bit extreme. Don't be afraid to experiment to see what works best for you. I have a pea stone walkway and I have found that simply rolling the project in the pea stones adds a nice distressed look. Even with the high cost of wood and hardware, it is highly recommended that you use the best lumber and hardware you can get. The difference in price between low cost, poor quality, and high cost, excellent quality, wood and hardware is really not very much, and using the better quality will enhance your finished project tenfold. The only really high cost factor in each of these projects is your time. For those who share a love for our past and our heritage and for Early American furniture, this cost is more than offset by the satisfaction derived from making future family heirlooms.

Part I

How to Build Colonial Furniture

The Antique Center at Hartland, Vermont.
Credit: Barbara E. Mills, Manager, The Antique Center at Hartland.

Origin of Colonial Furniture

Original country furniture was primarily utilitarian and made to fill a particular need. Country furniture was crafted at home by hand out of native woods, using primitive tools in most cases. Most of it was simple in design and quaint by today's standards. Despite its humble beginning, primitive and early Colonial furniture shows inspired creativity that distinguishes it; that is, it has a style of its own with enduring appeal. Today, 150- to 200-year-old designs are as beautiful as the day they were conceived.

It is the spirit of frank simplicity that gives Early American furniture its fundamental appeal. It naturally blends well with an open fire, wrought-iron hinges, hewn beams, and wide board flooring.

In 1798 Eli Whitney invented the cotton gin and made machinery to mass-produce identical parts for muskets. This revolutionary idea was the introduction of mass production. By 1808, Eli Terry, a Connecticut clock maker, signed a contract to make 4,000 wooden-geared clock works in two years. This was unheard of at that time. It took him one full year just to make water-powered machinery to mass-produce the parts for the clock works. He fulfilled the order of 4,000 works in the second year of the contract. Lambert Hitchcock started to mass-produce chairs as early as 1820. It is, therefore, reasonable to assume that an object from the early 1800s might possibly have been mass-produced.

WOODS

Different kinds of wood influenced the many styles of furniture. Queen Anne style is thought of as belonging to the "age of walnut"; mid 18th-century Georgian and American Colonial furniture styles to the "age of mahogany."

WHAT IS AN ANTIQUE?

Webster's New International Dictionary
"1. In general, anything very old . . . 2. A relic or object of ancient art . . . Belonging to the style or fashion of antiquity or a time long gone by . . . Among the oldest of its class."

Henry Morrison Flager Museum, Palm Beach, Florida
"An antique is at least 100 years old, reflecting the history of its time, both in design and economy."

Ann Gilbert, writer on Antiques
"An antique, in the purest sense, is a hand-crafted object, made before 1830, the dawn of the industrial, mass-produced object. Reproductions of these hand-crafted pieces are simple reproductions of antiques whether they were recreated in 1876 or 1976. Items made after 1830 should be classified according to the design period, i.e., Art Nouveau, Art Deco, or Moderne and Collectibles, etc.

U. S. Customs
"An antique is any item over 100 years old."

It should be noted, I feel, that furniture and accessories made between the time of the landing of the Mayflower and the dawn of the Industrial Revolution can be classified Colonial.

WHERE TO FIND ANTIQUES

Although most prices are very high, antiques can still be found. Perhaps the very best place to find an-

Richard Withington in action at one of his famous country auctions at Hillsboro, NH.
Credit: Photo by David Hewett for *Maine Antique Digest*.

Pictured is the charming village green in Grafton, Massachusetts, site of the Stephen Allman Promotions Annual Outdoor Antique Show.
Credit: *New England Country Antiques*.

tiques is at high-quality auctions. These are found throughout the East Coast area, especially New England. Antique shops are also excellent sources of early furniture and accessories. With the scarcity of Early American objects, many people are now buying antiques from Europe. Those brought from Europe are usually much larger, heavier, and more ornate than Colonial antiques of America. In the past few years, co-op antique shops have developed, where from twenty to three hundred dealers setup in one location. Flea markets also provide an excellent place to find all kinds of Early Americana—along with "early plastic" Americana.

Perhaps the best place to find low-priced antiques is at the Saturday yard sale. Many people setting up yard sales do not know the actual worth of what they have had up in the attic for years.

Regardless of where you find antiques, study them, note the finish, the wear marks and how it has been constructed, and try to make *your* projects look like these originals.

Essentials of Design

Three things of primary importance in the design of any piece of furniture are utility, strength, and of course appearance. Early craftsmen actually changed the basic designs from Europe to suit their own needs. Their designs were simpler and much more practical. They were built of local woods, rather than the established woods used in Europe.

One rather simple design feature associated with Colonial designs is the *cyma curve*. (See figure 1.)

The dictionary defines a cyma curve as "a projecting

CYMA CURVE

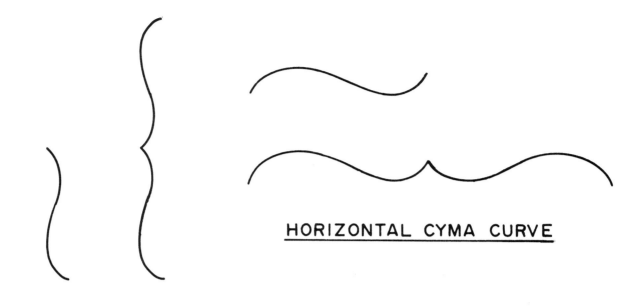

HORIZONTAL CYMA CURVE

VERTICAL CYMA CURVE

Figure 1

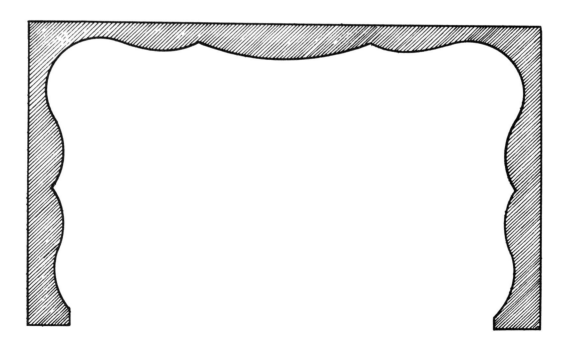

COMBINATION VERTICAL & HORIZONTAL CYMA CURVES

Figure 2

VARIATION

TURNING

Figure 3

molding whose profile is a double curve . . . formed by the union of a concave line and a convex line."

Colonial furniture used this graceful curve exquisitely and it is found in one form or another on almost all pieces—along the sides of hanging shelves, along the bottom aprons of stools or chests, and along the tops and sides of cabinets.

The cyma curve can be used vertically, horizontally, or both. (See figure 2.) It can be used with slight variations and on a lathe turning. (See figure 3.) It was the cyma curve that gave Colonial furniture its pleasing effect, its charm, and its warmth.

Basic Methods Used to Construct Colonial Furniture

Most projects in this book are built from several pieces held together by various kinds of joints. There are over three hundred recognized joints used today. However, the ones illustrated here are only those used in years past and those that were used for the projects in this text. If you do not have a shop full of the latest power tools, take heart; the craftsmen of yesterday, who built the original projects, had only crude hand tools at their disposal. If you do have power tools, by all means use them, but do not be intimidated if you do not have them. It is recommended, regardless of how many power tools you do have, that you *finish* each project by hand in order to add the subtle touches that give the handmade look of yesterday. Instructions will be given later on on how to add one hundred years to each project by hand-sanding "worn" edges and corners, how to shade areas where dirt would have accumulated over the years, and how to distress your project.

The strength and the appearance of each joint are extremely important. In years past, craftsmen did not rely on glue, but rather on the accuracy of tight-fitting joints.

An early cabinet maker from *The Panorama of Professions and Trades* magazine of 1836.
Credit: Old Sturbridge Village. Photo by Henry E. Peach.

JOINTS
Common edge joints

The three most common edge joints used in years past are the butt joint (see figure 4), the tongue and groove joint, and the rabbet joint. The simple butt joint was produced by butting one edge to another edge and gluing them together. The butt joint is commonly used where great strength is not important. By adding dowels to make a dowel joint (see figure 5), strength is added. If correctly made, the dowel joint will provide better alignment of mating parts. The dowel joint was *not* used in old projects; it is illustrated here only to suggest a method to use if more strength is needed for today's use of these projects. After the mating parts are assembled, the dowels will be hidden forever and the joint will appear to be an old butt joint.

A tongue and groove joint is an adaptation of a butt joint in which a tongue cut into one part fits into a groove of the mating part. (See figure 6.)

Another popular joint was the rabbet joint, originally called the rebate (pronounced "rabbit"). It was much stronger than the butt joint, as it provided a

EDGE JOINTS

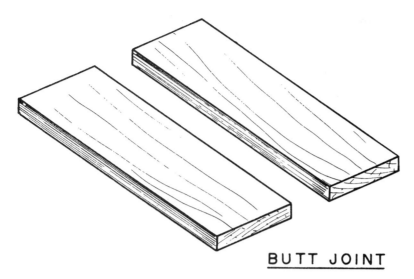

BUTT JOINT

Figure 4

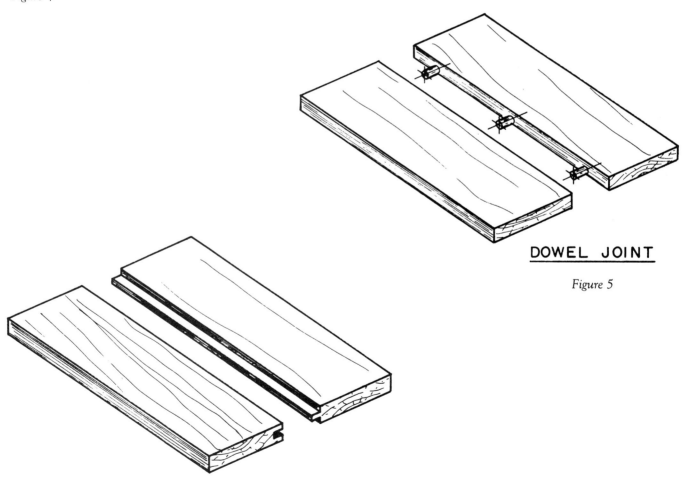

DOWEL JOINT

Figure 5

TONGUE & GROOVE JOINT

Figure 6

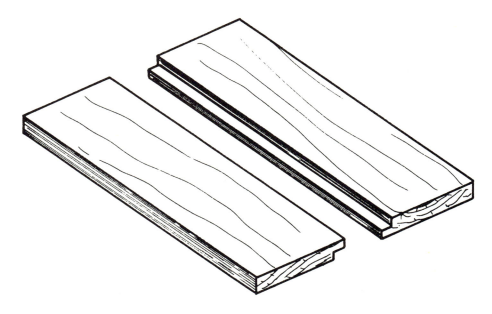

Figure 7   RABBET JOINT

larger gluing or nailing surface. (See figure 7.) As time goes by the joint may open up slightly, but no daylight will be seen at the joint.

Lap joints

A lap joint was used to extend the length of a member or to change direction of two pieces. Half of each part is cut away so that the surfaces between mating parts are flush when assembled. Three kinds of lap joints are the cross lap joint, middle lap joint, and end lap joint. (See figure 8.)

Surface joints

The surface joints used in making most of the projects throughout this book are the butt corner joint and butt tee joint (see figure 9); the rabbet joint (see figure 10); and the dado joint, half dovetail dado joint, and the full dovetail dado joint (see figure 11). The butt joint and butt tee joint were used in making most of the simple, "primitive" pieces. More formal pieces use the rabbet joint. Chests and chests of drawers use the dado, half dovetail dado, and full dovetail joints.

Mortise and tenon joints

Mortise and tenon joints are among the oldest joints and are very strong. As glue was not used much in Colonial days, the mortise and tenon joint was used in many places. In the original old pieces these joints are still as tight and strong as they were 150 years ago. The mortise and tenon joint was primarily used in leg and rail construction for tables, chairs, and benches. There are several kinds of mortise and tenon joints: the blind mortise and tenon joint, the through mortise and tenon joint, and the open corner mortise and tenon joint. (See figure 12.)

The original practice was to make the tenon about one-third to one-half the thickness of the thinner piece of the joint, with the width no more than six times the thickness of the tenon. Wide tenons tend to weaken the mortise.

Multiple tenon construction was used because it is much stronger than the single tenon. The space between multiple tenons must be at least equal to the thickness of the thinner piece.

Stub through mortise and tenon

A simple method to hold the mortise and tenon in place was the stub through method. A hole or holes were drilled through the mortise and tenon after assembly and a pin, or dowel, was inserted in each hole. Many projects in this text used this method of construction. With today's glue it probably is not necessary, but in order to have a more authentic finished project it is best to put them in for appearance sake. A dowel glued into a drilled hole will surface nicely and give that old look. (See figure 13.)

LAP JOINTS

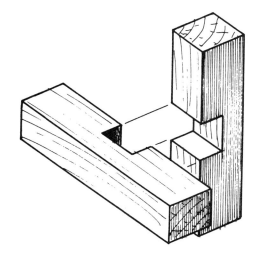

CROSS LAP JOINT

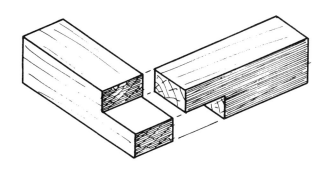

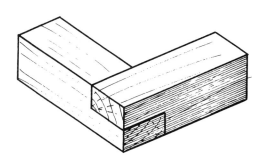

END LAP JOINT

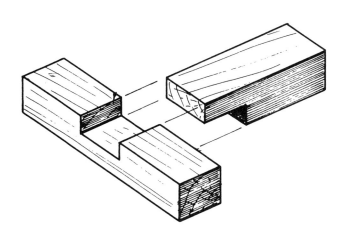

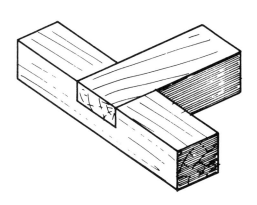

MIDDLE LAP JOINT

Figure 8

JOINTS

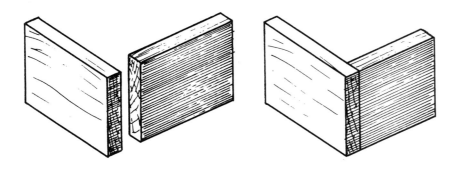
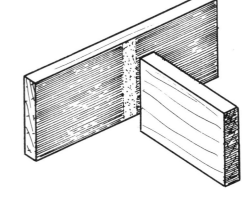

BUTT CORNER JOINT

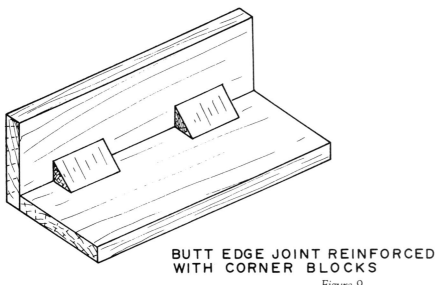

BUTT EDGE JOINT REINFORCED WITH CORNER BLOCKS

Figure 9

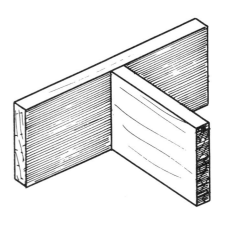

BUTT TEE JOINT

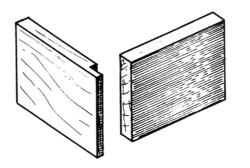
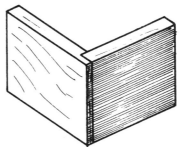

RABBET JOINT

Figure 10

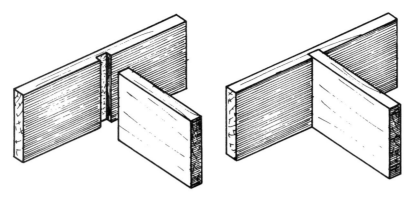

DADO JOINT

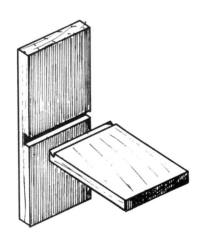 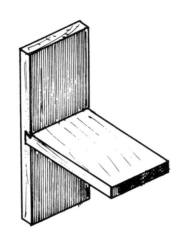

HALF DOVETAIL DADO JOINT

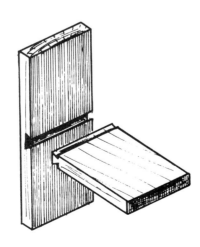 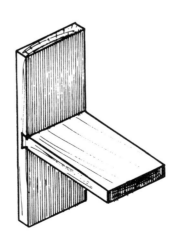

FULL DOVETAIL DADO JOINT

Figure 11

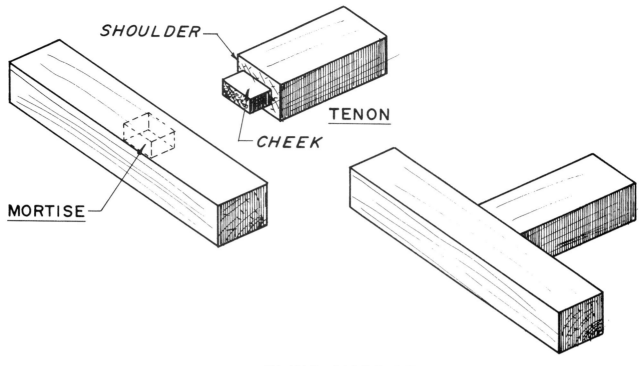

BLIND MORTISE & TENON

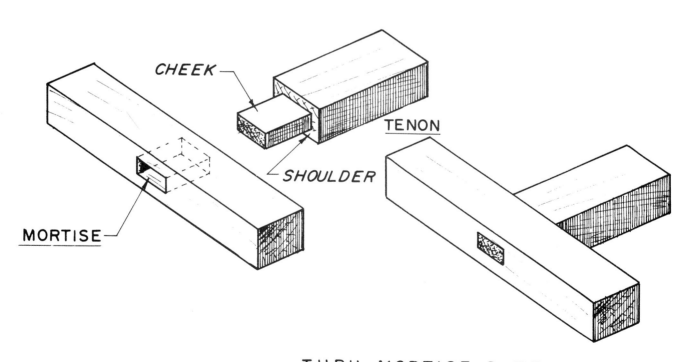

THRU MORTISE & TENON

Figure 12

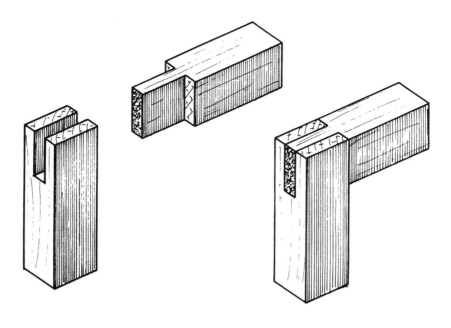

OPEN CORNER MORTISE & TENON

Figure 12

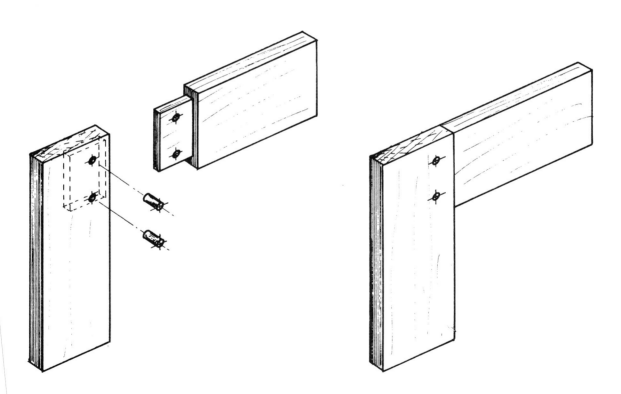

STUB THRU MORTISE & TENON

Figure 13

Drawbore pin

As glue was not used in making most early furniture, various other methods had to be used to hold parts together. The mortise and tenon joint was often used and compares to the best of today's glued joints. To ensure an extremely tight fit, the hole for the pin was located about 1/16 inch nearer the shoulder in the tenon than in the mortise. (See figure 14.) When the pin was driven into place, the tenon was drawn tightly up against the shoulder. This method or process was referred to as the drawbore pin method. It was used extensively in the construction in old barns and early homes.

Keyed mortise and tenon joints

The mortise and tenon joint goes all the way back to ancient Greece. Early benches and trestle tables were made with keyed mortise and tenon joints. This joint consists of a tenon that proceeds through and projects beyond the mortise member. The tenon is held in place by a tapered "key." This key can be fitted either horizontally or vertically. (See figure 15.) Because the key was tapered, the shoulder of the tenon was forced tightly against the mortised member, making an extremely tight fit. This joint was popular in the days when the table board (top) was removed from the table legs and the table was dismantled daily between meals.

Dovetail joints

The dovetail joint dates back five thousand years to Egyptian sarcophagi (large coffins). Today the dovetail joint is found only in the finest high-quality drawer and box construction. These fine joints were made and fit by hand. There are three major kinds of dove-

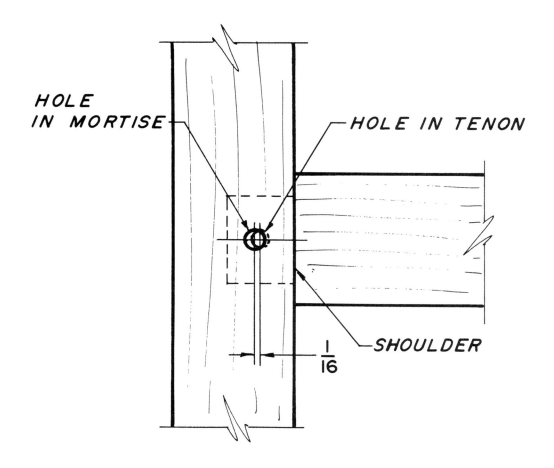

DRAWBORE PIN

Figure 14

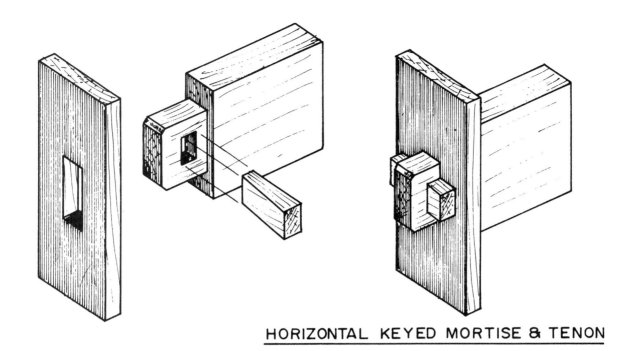

HORIZONTAL KEYED MORTISE & TENON

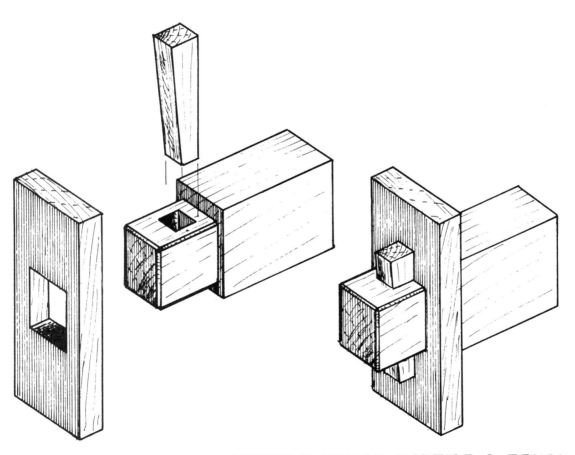

VERTICAL KEYED MORTISE & TENON

Figure 15

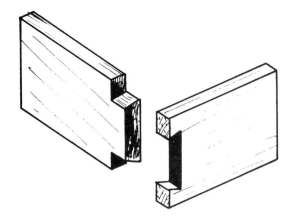
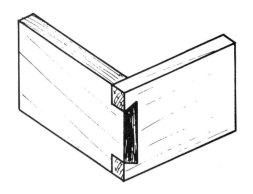

SIMPLE DOVETAIL

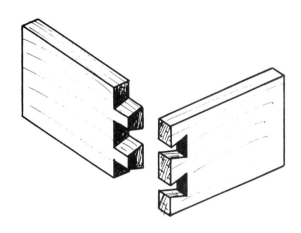
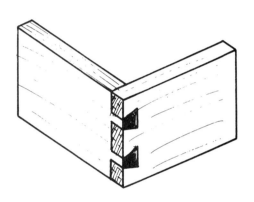

THRU DOVETAIL

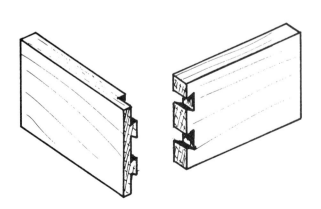
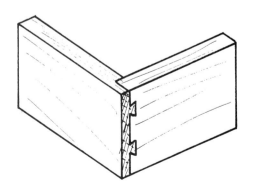

HALF BLIND DOVETAIL

Figure 16

tail joints used in this text: the simple dovetail, through dovetail, and the half blind dovetail. (See figure 16.) Dovetail joints of today are usually designed so that the pins are the same size as the tails and are made by a machine. The original method of having the pins wider than the tails was actually done because it makes a stronger joint. The usual angle for a dovetail is about 20°—10° either side of the center. (See figure 17.) To approximate this 10° angle, place a T-bevel square at a point 5 inches in and 1 inch over, as illustrated.

Exposed dado joints and dovetail joints express simple, honest design and construction.

Dado/plow cut

The dado and the plow cut are very similar except a dado is a notch cut across the grain of the wood; a plow is a notch cut with the grain of the wood. (See figure 18.)

Rabbet cut

The rabbet cut is used in many of the projects throughout this book. It was easier to make than cutting a 45° miter corner. The rabbet cut leaves a much smaller exposed edge joint than a simple butt joint. (See figure 19.)

CHAMFERED BEVEL EDGE

A corner cut at an angle is very pleasing to the eye, thus the chamfered edge was used. (See figure 20.) A corner cut at an angle to the other edge of the wood is a bevel cut. (See figure 21.)

MOLDINGS

Moldings are an important part of making Colonial furniture. (See figure 22.) In Colonial days moldings were made with multiple molding planes. Today, multiple molding planes can be used, but most moldings

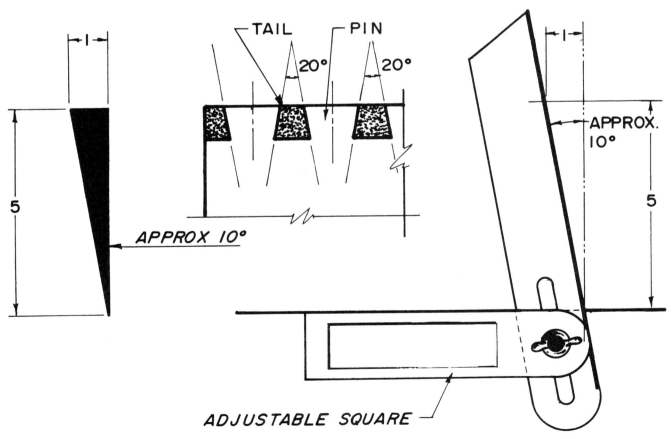

Figure 17

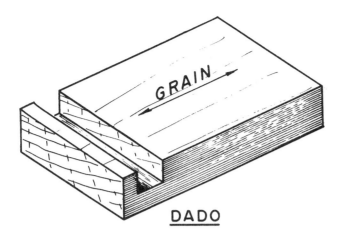
DADO

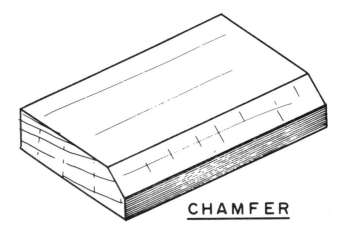
CHAMFER

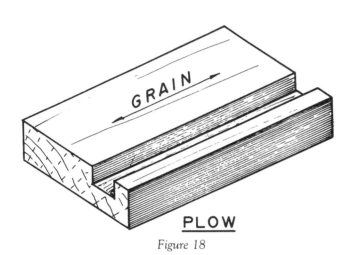
PLOW

Figure 18

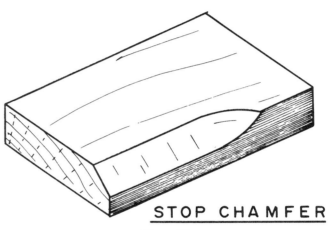
STOP CHAMFER

Figure 20

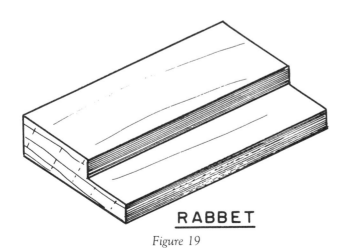
RABBET

Figure 19

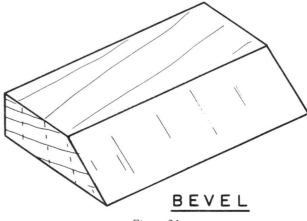
BEVEL

Figure 21

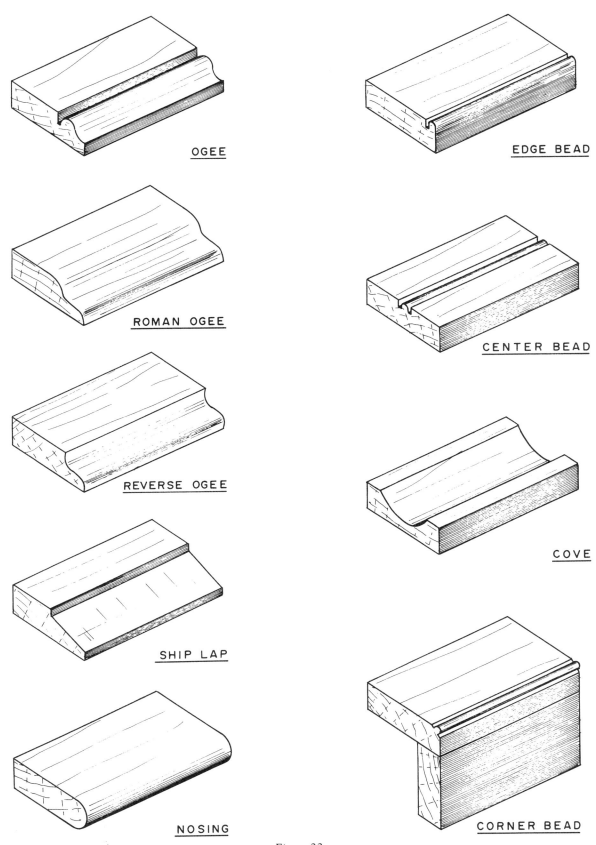

Figure 22

are made with router bits or shaper blades. Special moldings that cannot be made with standard router bits or shaper blades can be reproduced by a scratch beader. Some veteran woodworkers actually prefer using a scratch beader to obtain that "just right" molding. The scratch beader probably would not be a good tool for mass production but is excellent for one-of-a-kind projects.

A scratch beader is nothing more than an L-shaped piece of hardwood with a vertical saw kerf extending the entire length of the horizontal leg and partway into the vertical leg of the L. (See figure 23.) The vertical leg of the L has a rounded shoulder to enable it to follow along irregular or curved edges. Bolt holes are drilled along the saw kerf of the horizontal leg in order to hold the cutter blade in place. See figure 24 for a detailed plan of the scraper handle. The cutting blade is simply a piece of steel approximately 1/16 inch thick. Old scrapers, saw blades, or putty knife blades make good cutting blades. The cutting blade is cut, filed, or ground into a negative (opposite) profile of the molding profile needed. (See figure 25.) Be sure to add enough material to the cutting blade to fasten it to the handle securely. The actual cutting edge of the scratch beader should be tapered 3° to 5° as shown.

Start the cutting process with the blade protruding about 1/16 inch below the horizontal leg of the handle. Reset the cutter blade 1/16 inch deeper and make an-

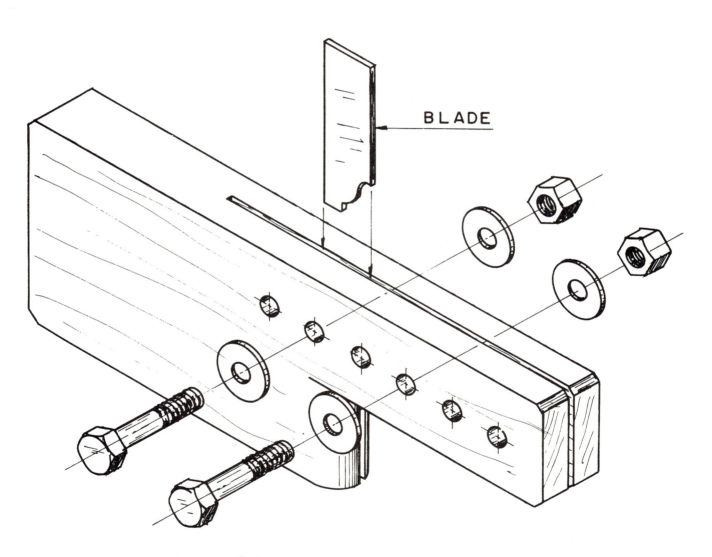

SCRATCH BEADER

Figure 23

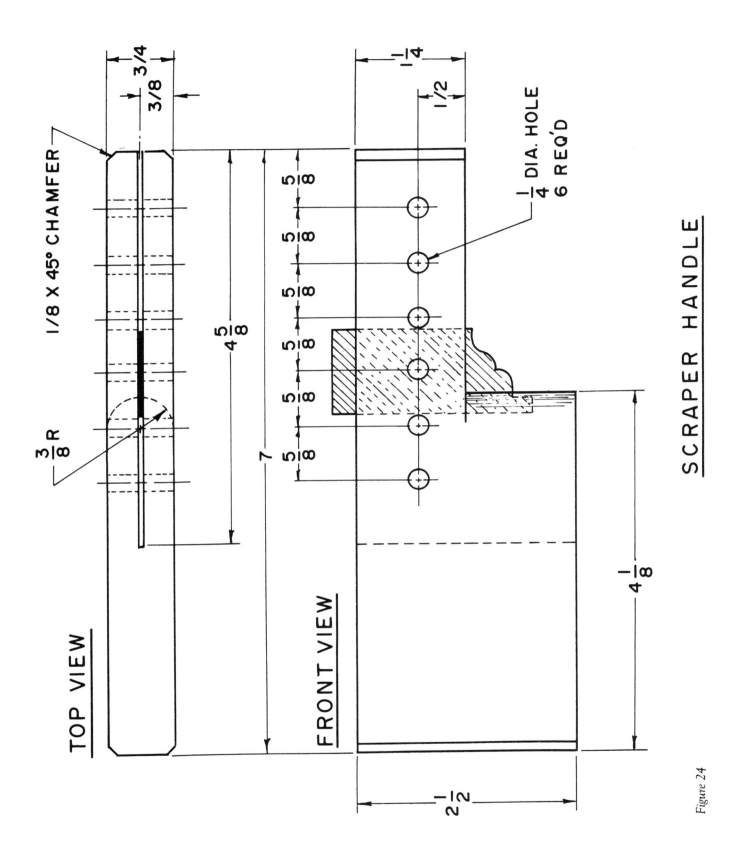

Figure 24

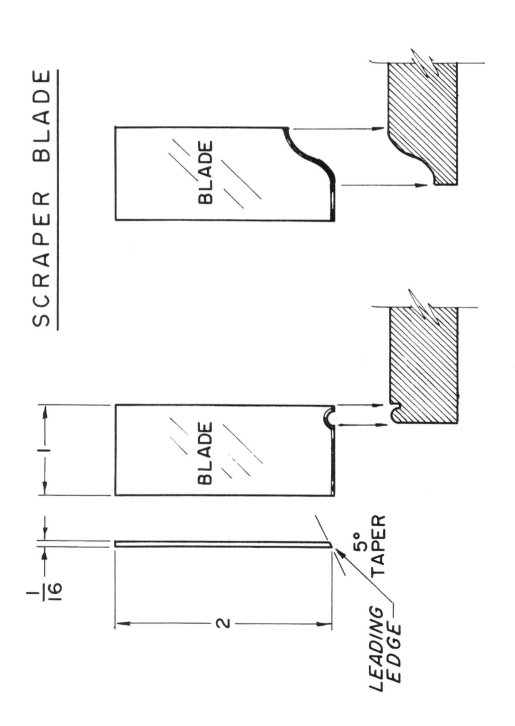

Figure 25

other pass. Repeat this until the desired profile is achieved. (See figure 26.)

Using the bead scraper is somewhat of an art and will become easier with practice. If the work is not 100% exact and a slight wave occurs it will *look* handmade—125 years ago.

The scratch beader can cut both with the grain and across the grain and will not tear the wood if used correctly. However, when getting near a corner it is a good idea to scrape *in* from the end to avoid chipping the end.

SAW-MADE MOLDINGS

Larger moldings with unusual shapes can be made with a table saw or a radial arm saw. Sketch the desired shape directly on the end of the stock or make a cardboard pattern and draw the desired shape on the end of the stock. (See figure 27.) By eye, adjust the height of the saw blade and adjust the saw fence accordingly in order to cut just below the inscribed line drawn at the end of the material. (See figure 28.) Keep adjusting the saw blade height and the saw fence and make various saw cuts, keeping just below the line. Complete the molding by sanding out the "steps" left by the saw blade cuts. (See figure 29.)

COVE CUTS

A deep radius cove can be cut using a table saw or radial arm saw. This technique involves passing the stock through the saw blade at an *angle* instead of parallel to the blade. Depending on the angle, anything from a wide circular cross section to an extremely narrow elliptical cove molding can be made. (See figure 30.)

Figure 26

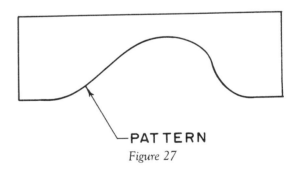

Figure 27

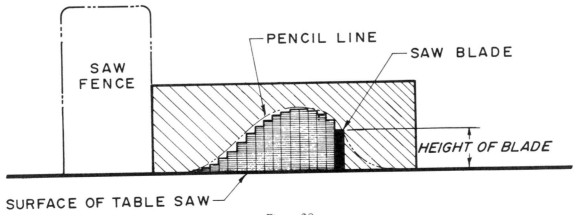

Figure 28

END OF BOARD

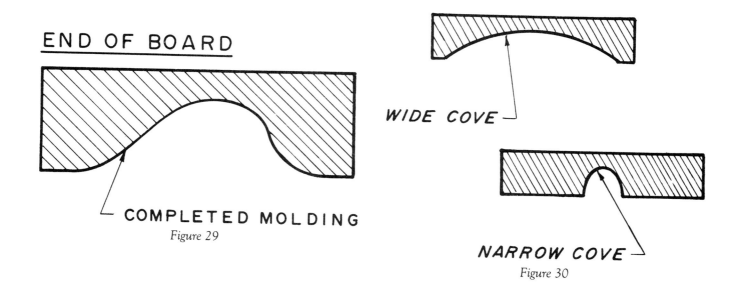

Figure 29 — COMPLETED MOLDING

Figure 30 — WIDE COVE / NARROW COVE

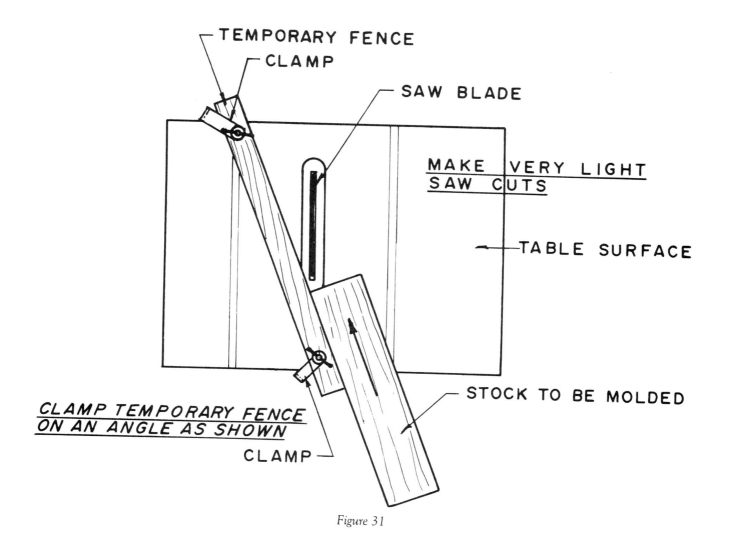

Figure 31

The table saw must be set as illustrated in figure 31. At the end of the stock sketch the desired profile. Set the saw blade so it extends up approximately 1/16 inch. Pass the stock across the saw blade, then raise the blade another 1/16 inch. Repeat these steps until the required cove is completed. It is a good idea to make smaller and smaller upward adjustments as the desired shape is achieved and pass the stock over the blade very slowly to achieve a smooth cove surface. A 60-tooth carbide combination saw blade will produce a smooth cove surface. (See figure 32.)

The radial arm saw makes this job even easier, as the blade can be simply set at an angle and the stock fed into it, using the regular fence.

A cove cut can be used to produce many kinds of moldings. (See figure 33.) Note the shape of the molding and the cove cut. To make molding like this simply make the desired cove cut (first cut). (See figure 34.) Set the saw blade at 45° and make the second cut on *both* sides, as shown. Turn the material over and with the saw blade still at 45°, make the third cut as shown on *both* sides. If the saw blade is set at exactly 45°, the two corresponding cuts will result in an exact 90° angle as shown in figure 33.

DRAWER CONSTRUCTION

Some projects in this text have drawers in them, either flush drawers or lip drawers. These drawers must slide in and out freely and easily. Most of the projects use the flush drawer. This is a drawer that fits into the opening of the case. The drawer edges do not extend beyond the case front. A flush drawer must be carefully made and fitted so the space between the drawer front and case is not excessive.

The lip drawer has a front edge that overlaps the actual opening in the case, thus hiding the space around the drawer. This kind of a drawer can be fitted a little loose, since this space is hidden.

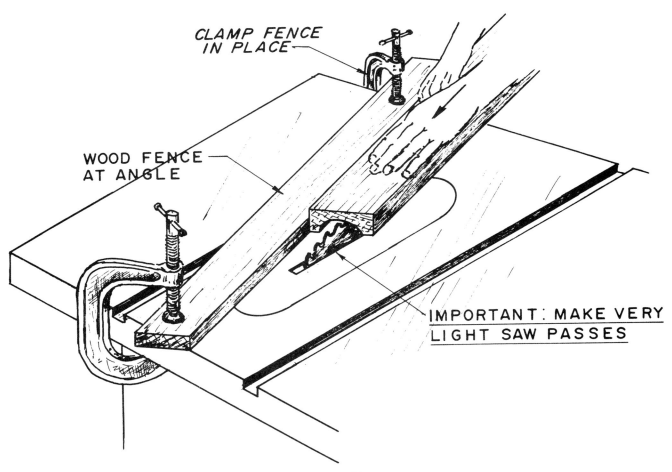

Figure 32

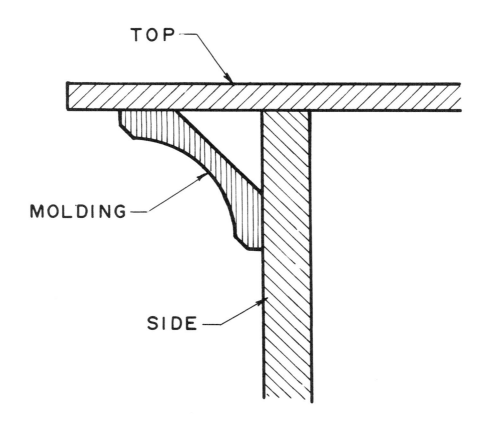
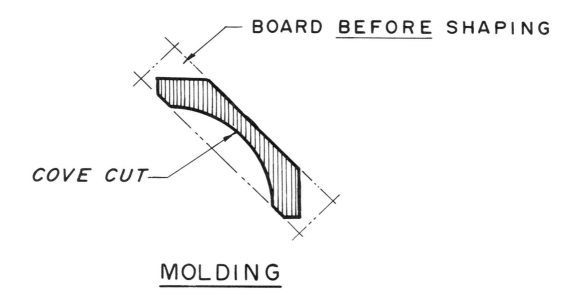

Figure 33

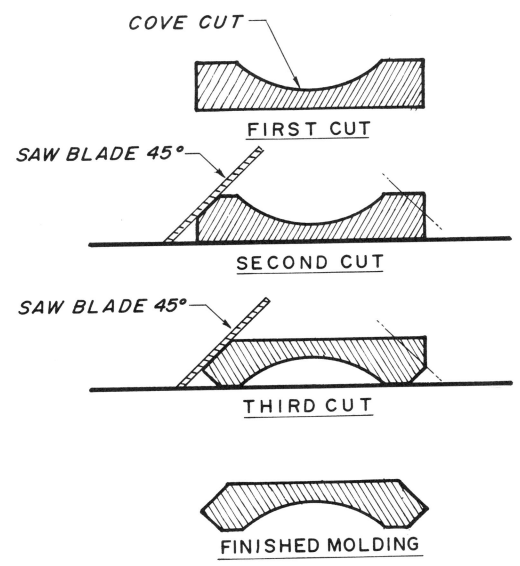

Figure 34

Early drawers were either rabbeted or dovetailed, as seen in figures 35 and 36.

A drawer is simply a box without a top, made up of the front, the two sides, the back, and the bottom. (See figure 37.) In most all Early American furniture, the drawer bottom was made of thick material and its bottom surface was feathered thinner along all four sides. (See figure 38.) This feathering can be done with a cove cut on a table saw or radial arm saw. A similar effect can be achieved with a hand plane to make a chamfer with an angle of about 10°.

To determine the required size of the drawer, carefully measure the drawer opening into which the drawer will be going. Record the height, width, and depth of the opening. Make the drawer itself about $1/32$ to $1/16$ inch less than the recorded opening height, and about $1/16$ to $3/32$ inch less than the recorded opening width. Make the drawer about $1/16$ to $1/8$ inch shorter than the recorded depth.

Choose the wood for the drawer front carefully. It should match the rest of the project and have an interesting grain pattern.

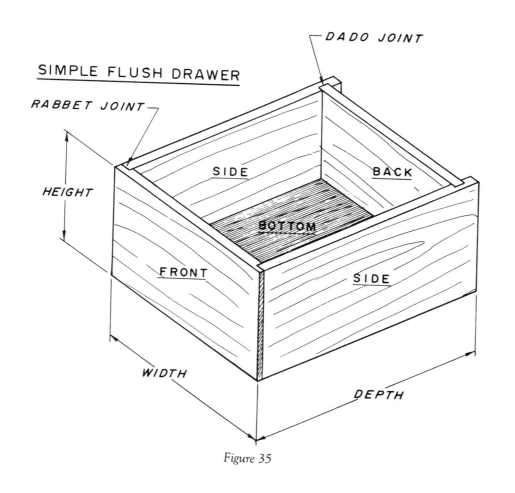

Figure 35

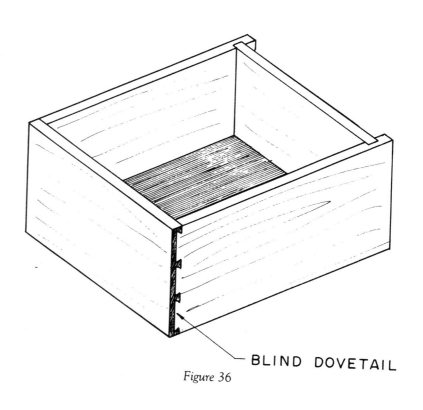

Figure 36

SIMPLE FLUSH DRAWER

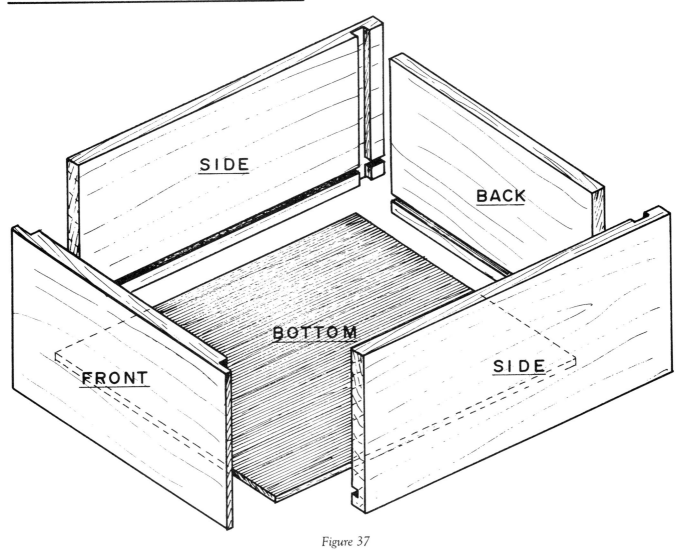

Figure 37

The front piece should be slightly thicker than the other parts. Usually the front is ¾ inch thick with sides, back, and bottom about ½ to ⅝ inch thick. The sides, back, and bottom should be made of a secondary wood.

DRAWER SUPPORTS

Furniture of today has drawer guides, drawer rollers, and runners, all designed to make the drawer open and close smoothly. Drawer supports were very simple in furniture of yesterday. (See figure 39.) The rails between drawers are held in place with dado or dovetail joints. Drawer supports are no more than narrow rails with dado joints into side members—no elaborate drawer guides or rollers. Some smaller drawer openings used a solid board that acted as both the rail and support.

TABLE TOPS

Table tops and similar tops were held in place by four or eight simple blocks with two or three countersunk holes for flathead screws. (See figure 40.)

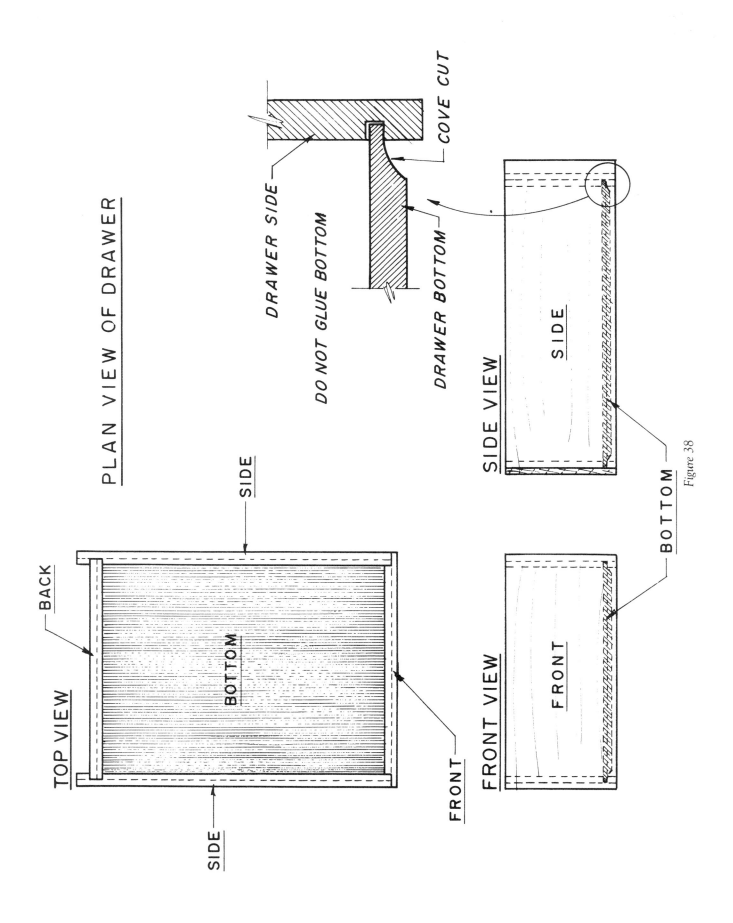

Figure 38

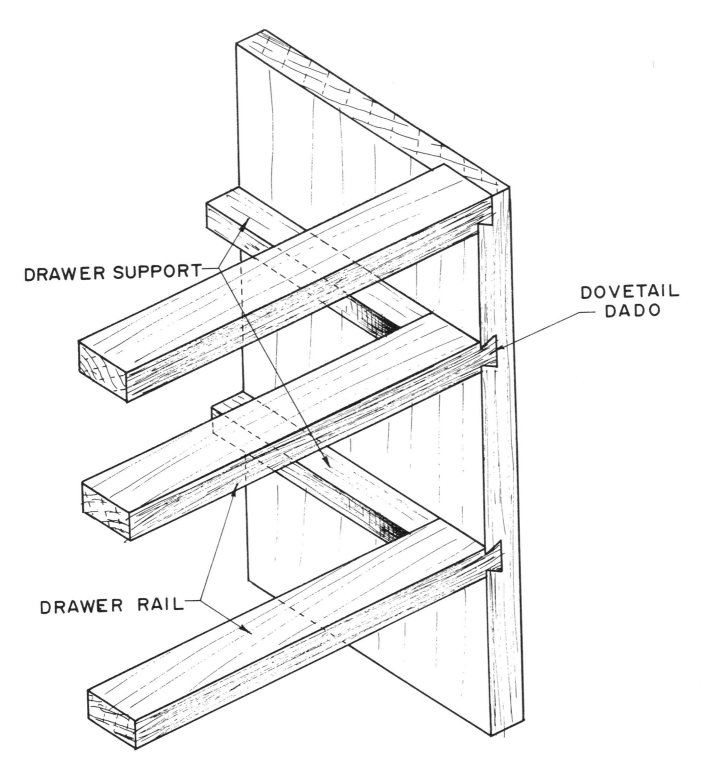

DRAWER SUPPORT DETAIL

Figure 39

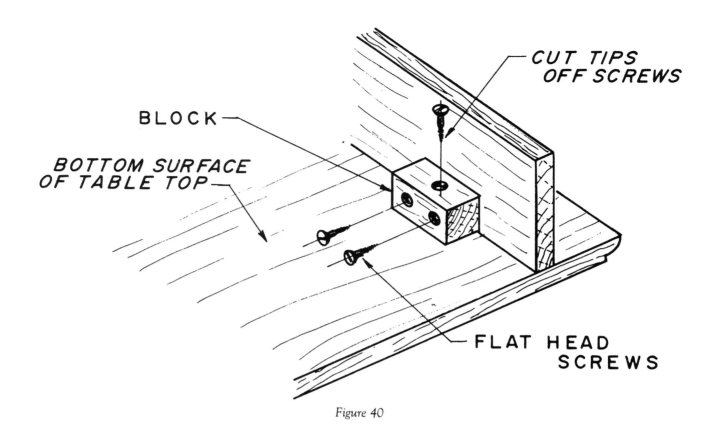

Figure 40

To Enlarge a Pattern

All curves and irregular shapes are illustrated in this book with a grid over them; in most cases a ½- or 1-inch-square grid is used. To enlarge these shapes, simply draw a full-size grid as noted on the plan. This can be done on a sheet of wrapping paper. To keep track of where you are, label the squares on the plan A-B-C-D-E-F etc. along one direction and 1-2-3-4-5-6 etc. along the other. (See Figure 41.) On the *full-size* grid drawn on the sheet of paper, label each square the same way. Locate a point on the original drawing and find and mark its exact location on the sheet of paper. Continue locating points on the original drawing and marking them on the full-size grid. Connect the dots and the pattern is full-size!

TRANSFERRING THE PATTERN TO THE WOOD

The full-size pattern can be transferred to the wood by one of three methods:

1. Place a sheet of carbon paper under the full-size pattern and trace the design.

2. Cut out the full-size pattern, place it on the wood, and trace around it.

3. If you plan to make many copies, make a plywood template. Be sure to write on it what the template is for, for use in years to come.

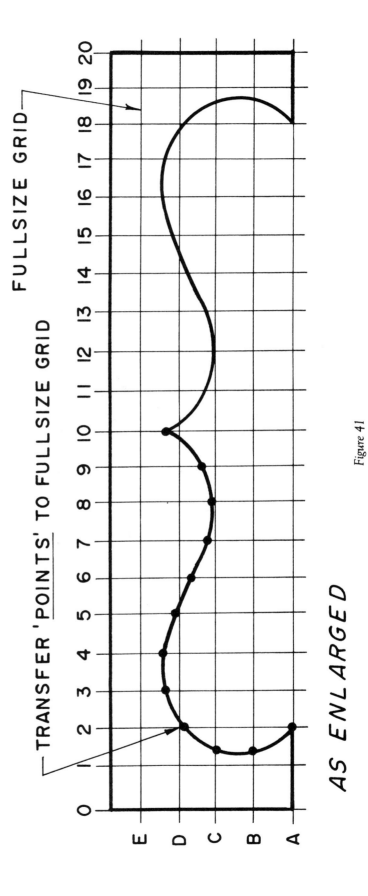

Figure 41

Colonial Hardware

SCREWS

Early screws were handmade of brass or iron. Screws made between 1690 and 1775 had blunt ends instead of points, the heads were not round, and the spirals were not even. The slot in the head of the screw was also very shallow. Machines to make screws were developed about 1790. These screws also had flat tips but the spirals were even. The slot, however, was still very shallow. By 1850 or so modern machines were developed to make screws more or less like those of today, with sharp tips, even spirals, and deep slots in the head. (See figure 42.)

NAILS

From ancient times, all nails were square with slightly larger heads and blunt ends. Wrought iron nails were handmade one at a time until 1790. Since then nails have been made by machines.

During the Colonial period, nails were an important commodity. The scarcity of nails in Colonial Virginia was reflected in a law enacted in 1645 to prohibit settlers from burning down old buildings for their nails. Some nails were made in the colonies in the seventeenth and eighteenth centuries but most were imported during that time.

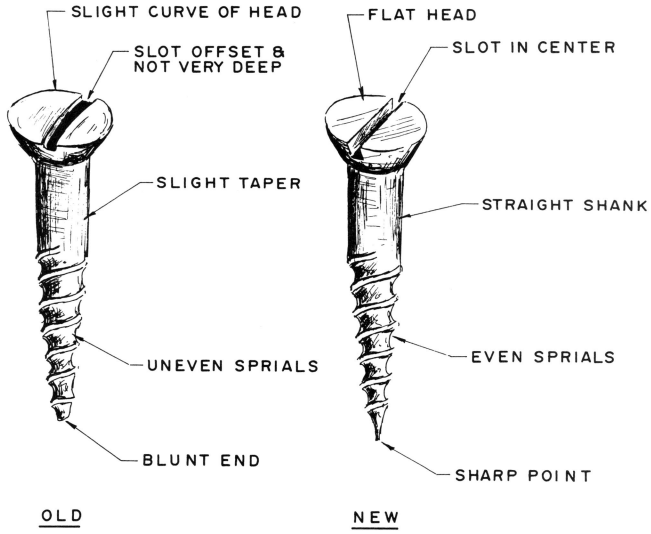

Figure 42

During and after the Revolution, America became dependent upon local sources for nails. Wrought nail rods were cut and forged by hand into nails. Later, nail plate was made in rolling mills to a uniform thickness and width, depending on nail size. Nails were cut to size by a machine that wiggled back and forth as the nail plate was fed into the reciprocating shear blade. (See figure 43.) This wiggling of the nail plate created a tapered nail with burrs and shear marks on diagonal edges. (See figure 44.) One end was heated in the forge, then pointed on four sides on the anvil. It was then placed into a hole of a particular size and depth that allowed the blunt end to project about ¼ inch. This projection was hammered down and spread, thus forming the head of the nail. These hammer blows created roundish crests. (See figure 45.) Some early machine-cut nails with handmade heads are illustrated in figure 46.

Sprigs and brads

These names were often confused or used inconsistently, but they generally refer to headless, L-head, or T-head nails. Smaller sizes were usually called sprigs, were from ½ to 2 inches in length and were usually sold by quantity. Larger sizes were usually called brads, 4d to 24d, and were usually sold by weight.

The square-cut nail has four cutting edges. When it's driven, the fibers of the wood press firmly against those four edges with a kind of wedge effect and much more holding power.

Square-cut nails should be used in making the projects throughout this book for that "authentic" construction look of Colonial days. In Wareham, Massachusetts, the Tremont Nail Company is still in existence, making exact copies of the square-cut nails of yesterday. The Wareham Company started in the Tre-

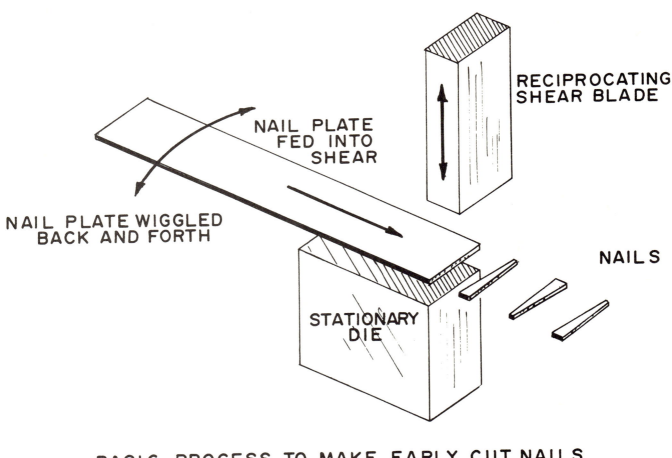

BASIC PROCESS TO MAKE EARLY CUT NAILS

Figure 43

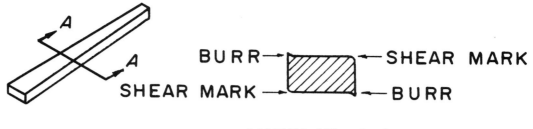

VIEW AT A-A

"WIGGLED" NAILS PRODUCE NAILS WITH BURRS AND SHEAR MARKS ON DIAGONAL EDGES

Figure 44

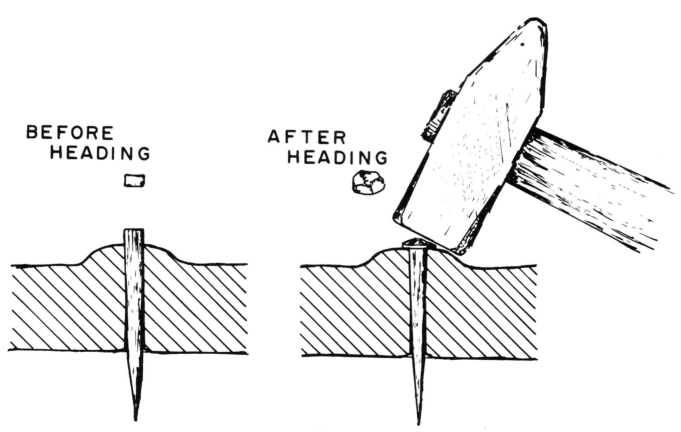

Figure 45

EARLY MACHINE-CUT NAILS WITH HANDMADE HEADS

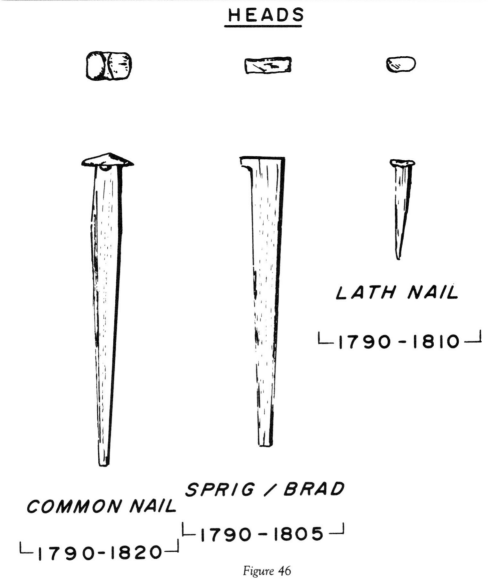

Figure 46

mont section of the town in 1819. In 1840 the current building was built on the site of a fulling mill that was burned by a British raiding party during the war of 1812. Today visitors to the factory find a throwback to New England industries of past years. (See figure 47.) Overhead shafts and belts drive the machinery that was once powered by water. The store, listed on the National Register of Historical Places, is now open to the public throughout the year and carries a full range of antique-style nails, hardware, and cooperage products. Over 165 years old, this company is one of the oldest in the United States making the same product in the same manner in the same buildings and at the same location—truly a test of time.

From penny-weight to penny

Originally the terms *8d* and *10d* (the small *d* indicated penny) were used to denote prices of nails per hundred. Due to the fluctuation of prices, this significance has been lost through the years. Today, this term is used to designate size. For example, a 2d nail is 1 inch long, an 8d nail is 2½ inches long, and a 100d nail is 8 inches long.

37

Figure 47

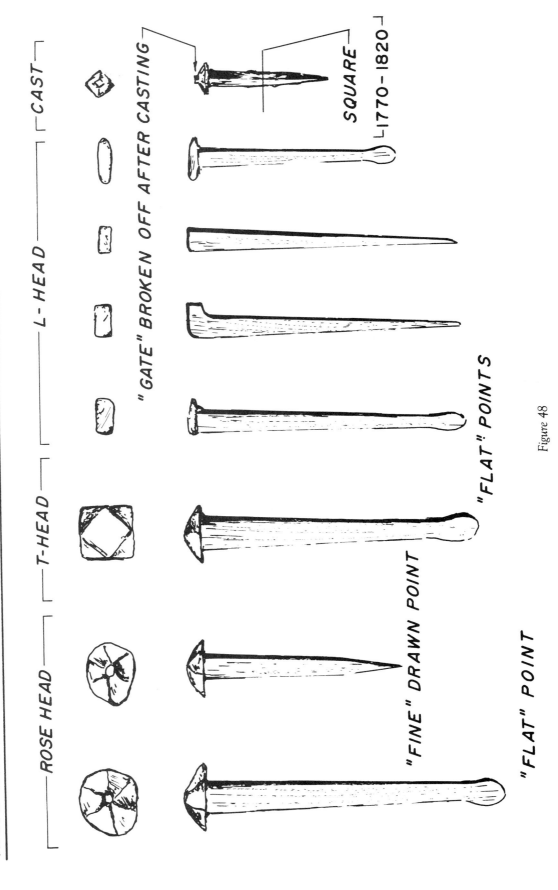

Figure 48

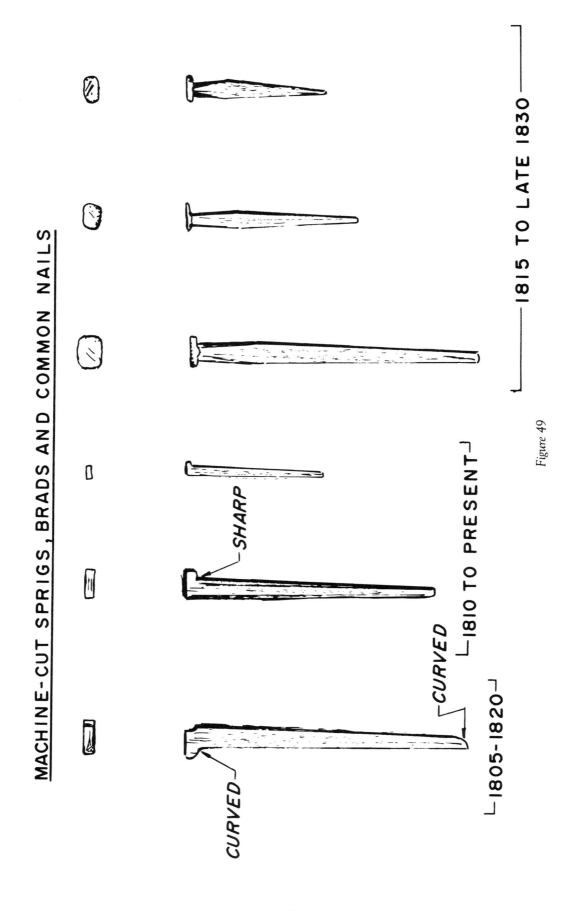

Figure 49

Various hand-wrought nails used from the seventeenth century up to the early nineteenth century are illustrated in figure 48. These nails were generally used for trim. With heads countersunk and puttied, they were also used for flooring. Other characteristics of hand-wrought nails: shanks usually tapered on both faces; iron fibers run lengthwise; lack of uniformity (especially heads).

Machine-cut sprigs, brads, and common nails are illustrated in figure 49. Curved corners and points are characteristic of this type.

Nails of this period are distinguished by their irregular heads, which vary in size and shape and are usually eccentric to shank, though they were more uniform by the 1830s. Nails were irregular in length and width, but more uniform at the end of this period. Nails generally have a rather distinct rounded shank (under head), caused by a wide heading clamp. These nails were more readily available than finishing nails and were often locally modified by hammering the sides of the heads, thus making them into finish nails, which could be countersunk.

Handmade nails were strong and tough. Because they were made of pure iron they were also highly rust-resistant.

Thomas Jefferson purchased a machine in 1756 to produce nails for sale. One of the earliest cut-nail machines was built by William J. Folsome at Harrisburg, Pennsylvania, in 1789. Folsome, originally from New Hampshire, was making 120,000 nails per week.

"Modern" machine-cut nails of today tend to be uniform in size and shape. (See figure 50). Nails manufactured at the Tremont factory today are very similar to those of the past and are recommended for use in the projects throughout this book. (See figure 51.)

Round nails, or wire nails, were first made in the

"MODERN" MACHINE-CUT NAILS

FINISH NAIL

COMMON NAIL

BOX NAIL

└──────── 1830 TO PRESENT ────────┘

Figure 50

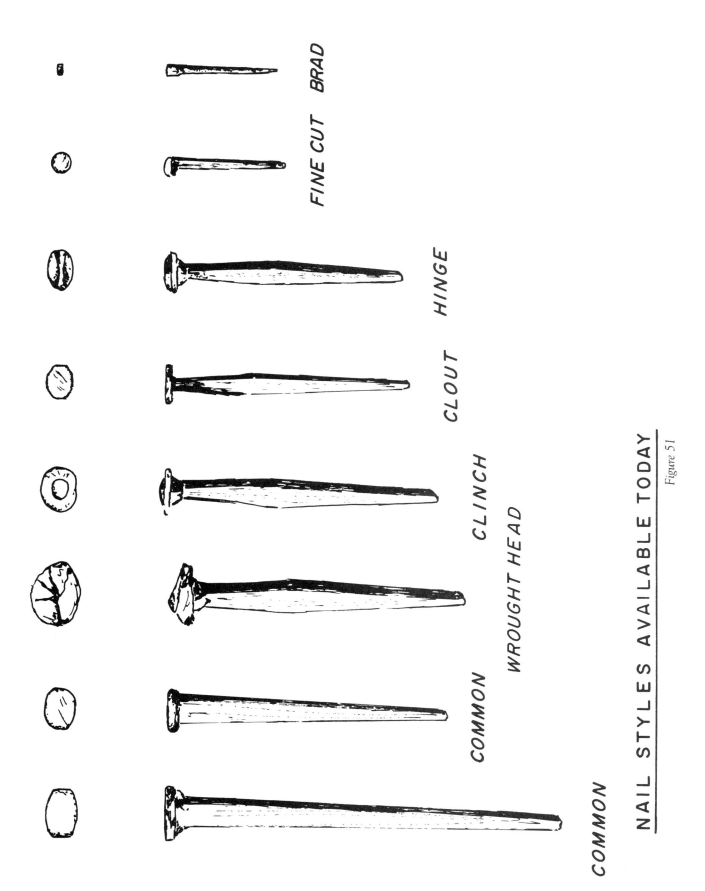

NAIL STYLES AVAILABLE TODAY

Figure 51

42

1850s. They were produced from machines imported from Europe. Early wire nails were not made for building construction, but rather in small sizes for pocketbook frames, cigar boxes, and the like.

The transition from cut nails to round nails was very gradual. Wire nails did not really become the major type until after 1895. Many builders preferred using cut nails into the twentieth century. Wire nails were easier, quicker, and cheaper to make. Round nails are also easier to drive, but the cut nail has much more holding power. Today cut nails are only used to nail tongue and groove flooring in position. They are unsurpassed for this and, once in place, create a very firm floor.

BRASSES

Today brass hardware is made four ways: cast, forged, extruded, or stamped. The cast and forged hardware best copies the original antique brasses. This hardware costs more, but looks much better and is much stronger. No other hardware has the ageless warmth and attractiveness that solid brass does. Brass ages well and complements wood tones beautifully.

Cast brass

Cast hardware is used for heavy pieces where a thick section is needed. Cast hardware includes hinges, drawer pulls, knobs, and handles. The cast process involves pouring molten brass into a mold made of sand, allowing it to cool, removing it from the sand, and then carefully polishing it to a high luster.

Forged brass

Forged hardware is the process whereby a red-hot piece of brass is shaped between two forging dies. One die is stationary and the other is attached to a drop hammer. The hot piece of brass becomes very plastic under the pressure of the drop hammer and flows into the voids of the die cavity. It too is removed from the forging dies and polished.

Extruded brass

The extruded brass process is similar to squeezing toothpaste out of a tube. With extrusion, a hot piece of brass is forced through a die of a particular shape. This process is used to make hinges, bolt parts, rods—anything that has a constant cross section. The extrusion process has a tendency to harden the brass, which makes it strong.

Stamped brass

An inexpensive method of making brass parts is the stamping process. In this method, a sheet of brass is stamped, cold, into various shapes.

Brass finishes

Brass hardware of today is either hand polished with a baked coat of clear lacquer added to protect its finish or "tumbled" in a container to give a nice finish. The "tumbled" brass hardware does not match the hand-polished process. (See figure 52.)

Escutcheon pins

Most old hardware was held in place by either brass, flathead, slotted screws or by escutcheon pins. To make your project "authentic," cut about 1/8 inch off the tips of the screws to match the original old handmade screws. Escutcheon pins were simply round-headed brass nails.

As a rule the brass escutcheon was chosen to complement the handles or drawer pulls. Very rarely did the escutcheon serve as a major design element. The size of the escutcheon was determined by the key size used with it. (See figure 53.)

Mounting the brasses

Most traditional knobs used in these projects are held in place by a brass screw. Take care always to drill a pilot hole before screwing the knob in place. Brass screws are not as strong as today's steel screws and could break off during the assembly process. Properly installed, these knobs should not loosen in normal use. Today, brass-plated screws are more available than solid brass screws.

When nuts and bolts are used, as with the drawer pulls, the bolt should be cut slightly shorter than the combined thicknesses of the drawer front and the nut. This is done so that the nut will thread onto the bolt, but the end of the bolt will not protrude past the nut. This is especially important in drawers that contain clothing as it will prevent snagging the drawer contents.

Note: Before cutting a bolt, thread the nut beyond the cut, so undoing the nut will smooth out the cut threads.

PULLS AND HANDLES

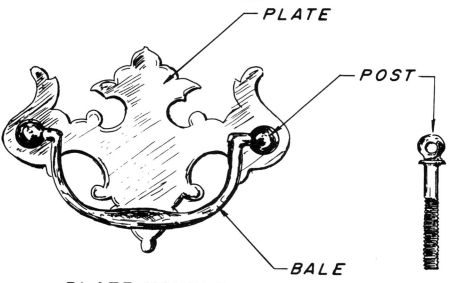

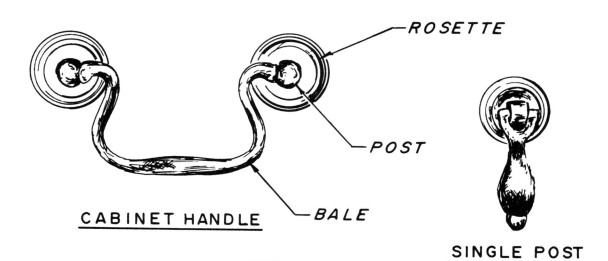

Figure 52

BRASS ESCUTCHEONS

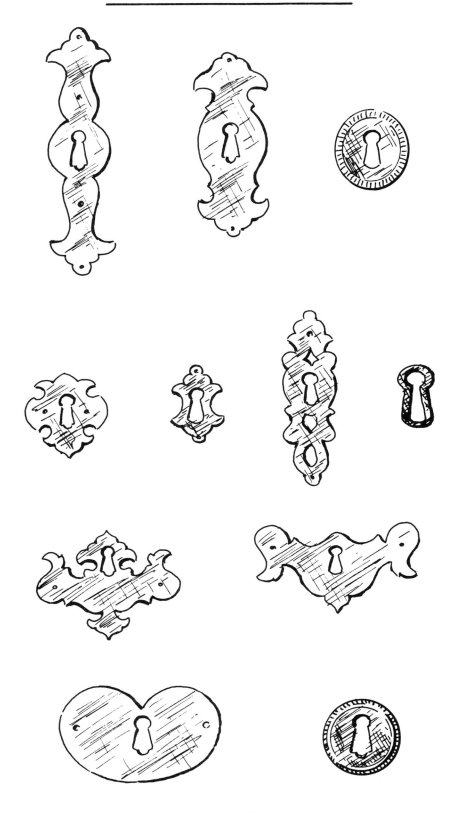

Figure 53

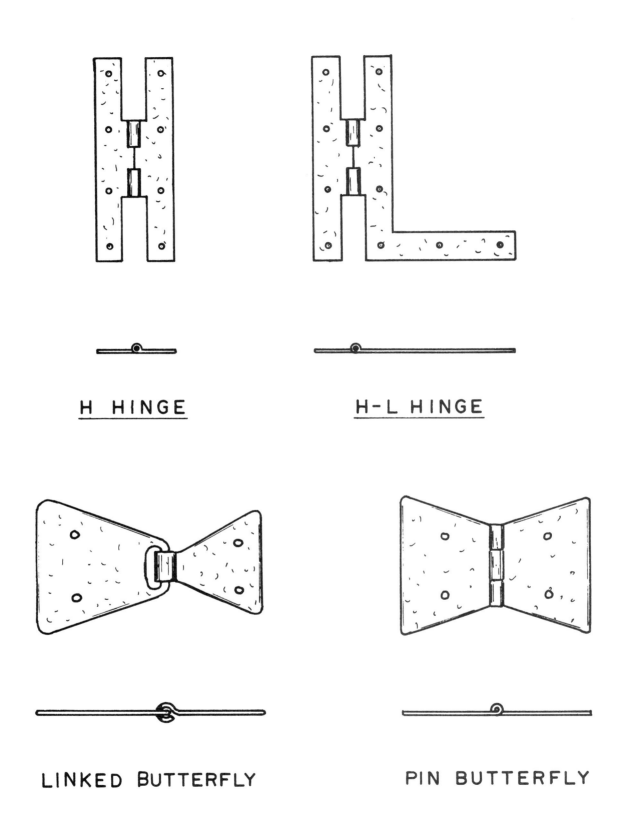

Figure 54

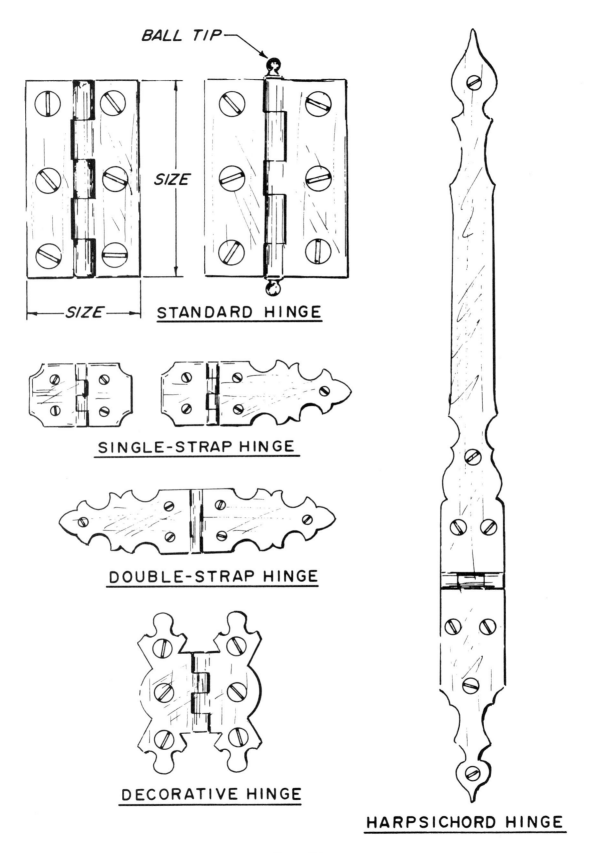

Figure 54

STRAP HINGE

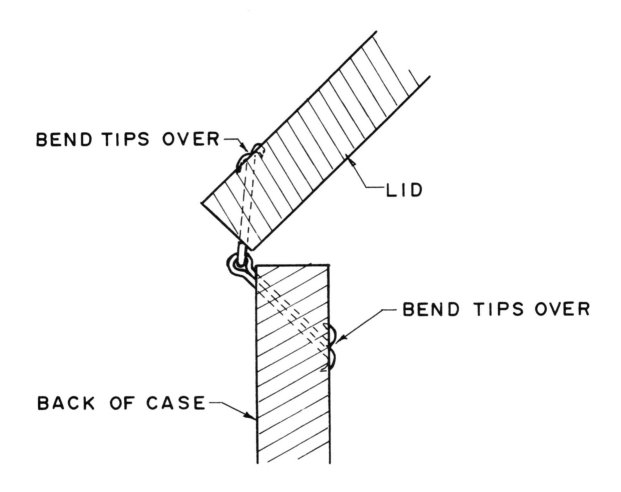

STRAP HINGE

Figure 54

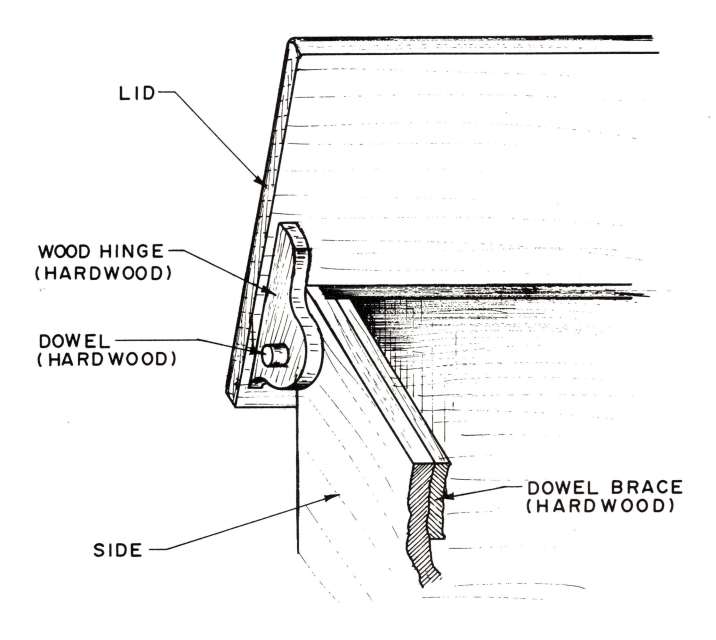

Figure 54

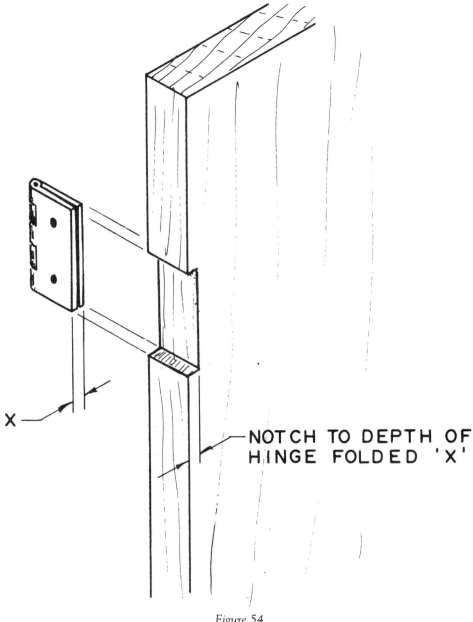

Figure 54

HINGE SIZES AND KINDS

Hinge sizes are noted by their height first and by their *open* width. A hinge listed as 1 x 2 is 1 inch high and 2 inches wide in its *open* state, or 1 inch wide closed.

Hinges can be cast, extruded, or pressed. The cast hinge is usually the heaviest. They are cast first and the hole and notches machined later. These hinges are used mostly for their solidity and aesthetic appeal. The extruded hinge looks similar to the cast hinge but tends to wear much longer, due to the natural hardening from the extruding process. Pressed hinges are the most inexpensive. The knuckles are firmed by bending the brass around a steel pin. As a rule, it is better to invest the difference in price and use cast or extruded hinges. These best duplicate the original antique hinges. (See figure 54.)

Patina

The aging process of wood causes the wood color to deepen. This is called patina. Patina adds beauty—the beauty of age—and is almost impossible to add to a newly constructed piece of country or primitive furniture. Under "Finishing Your Project," below, various ideas and suggestions will be given for you to try to add a little "age" to your project. A recipe you might try for creating "new" patina consists of ammonia and plug-tobacco, blended together and allowed to stand for ten days. Paint over raw wood.

Finishing Your Project

As a general rule, it should take you as long to finish a project as it did to make the project. If it took you six hours to make an object it should take you six hours to finish it. The finishing part is the most important, as *this* is what people see.

After a project has been made, carefully fill in all visible cracks between mating parts with water putty and sand the project, starting with a medium sandpaper and working up to a fine sandpaper (from 100 to 400 grit paper). Be sure to use a sanding block in order to achieve flat surfaces and sharp, crisp corners. For that "aged" look, distress your project by lightly tapping here and there on it with various objects or tools—even add scratches. I find rolling the project in pea stones or similar stones gives an excellent random series of "worn" marks. Think of how the project would have been used for the last hundred or so years and round some edges or corners where they would have been worn through the years from regular use. On a drawer, for example, the wear spots would be on the *bottom* of the two side boards and along the *top inside* of the front board. After distressing and rounding edges, resand lightly, using 400 grit paper. Finish up with #0000 steel wool. Do not be afraid to experiment. The distressing process will give your project that authentic look and be well worth the effort. Nothing looks worse than a reproduced "antique" that looks new!

Clean the entire work area and allow plenty of time for all dust to settle. Carefully wipe the project with a clean cloth with a little turpentine on it to remove all dust.

PAINT

No other early product demonstrates more clearly the ingenuity and adaptability of the Colonial American craftsman than milk paint. For the craftsman away from population centers, the availability of drying oils, varnish, and commercial pigments was limited and the cost was high. It is easy to see why these craftsmen turned to milk paint and earth colors or brick dust as an answer to their problem.

Milk paint is available today and two addresses where it may be obtained are listed in the Appendix. (See "Milk Paint" in "Antique Hardware and Accessories Suppliers.")

If you wish to be a purist, here is an early recipe: ½ gallon of skimmed milk, 6 ounces of lime, and 4 ounces of color. This formula gave a finish that was very coarse and dull in color. Through the years, this paint hardened, which makes it almost impossible to remove today.

The most authentic colors I have found manufactured today are by the Stulb Paint and Chemical Co. of Norristown, Pennsylvania. They manufacture a brand of paint under the name of Old Village Paint Colours and have developed colors that capture the spirit and character of Colonial, Federal, and Victorian periods. These colors are unique, lead-free, and of superb quality. Their address is listed in the Appendix. (See "Paint" in "Antique Hardware and Accessories Suppliers.")

Figure about 40 to 50 square feet per pint, 90 square feet per quart, and 400 square feet per gallon.

TO APPLY PAINT

Apply a coat of undercoat and allow to dry thoroughly; sand lightly with #0000 steel wool; and apply finish coat, following suggested instructions on the can. Allow to dry thoroughly.

To "age" your project, lightly sand all edges with #400 sandpaper wherever you think the project would

An old salt box. Notice the peeled paint and worn edges.
Credit: Old Sturbridge Village. Photo by Henry E. Peach.

have been normally worn throughout the years. This should be done wherever you sanded the edges after distressing. Sand down to the bare wood in some cases. Don't worry if some of the undercoat shows through. This would have happened through years of normal use.

WASH COAT

Completely wipe the project with a damp cloth to remove all dust. While waiting for this to dry thoroughly, mix up a "wash" coat of one part turpentine and one part black paint (or any other color). Wipe the wash coat over the entire project, especially in the corners and into the distress marks and scratches. This will bring out the distress marks and scratches. Wipe the entire project with a clean cloth, taking care to leave extra color in the corners to give an aged look to your work. If you apply too much, remove it in various places with a cloth and turpentine. Again, don't be afraid to experiment—you really can't go wrong. Study various antiques and note how they have aged. Note where and how they have been distressed throughout the years and try to duplicate this, being sure to use authentic colors.

TO APPLY STAIN

There are many good stains on the market; several are listed in the Appendix. Be sure to use a stain tint that was actually used years ago by early craftsmen, such as Ipswich pine, Early American, or walnut. If you are using softwood, such as pine, seal the wood with a light coat of tung oil before staining. Rub it into the wood and wipe off excess. (Hardwood should never be sealed before staining.)

Apply the stain following the suggested instructions on the can. After the stain is thoroughly dry, apply a coat of tung oil. (Tung oil is used, as it allows the wood to "breath" and will age faster to bring out a beautiful patina in time.)

Add the wash coat, just as you would if the surface were painted, to bring out the distress marks and allow to dry fully. Add two or three more thin coats of tung oil until you achieve the satin finish you want. Lightly rub with #0000 steel wool, wipe clean, and apply a coat of lemon oil. This penetrates the wood and keeps it from drying out. Never apply a paste wax to tung oil—this stops the "breathing" action of the wood.

Part II

Antique Shelf or Counter Projects

Mortars and Pestles

These were used to grind grains and spices. They were turned out of hardwoods such as maple, walnut, and ash.

MORTAR AND PESTLE
Walnut—natural finish

MORTAR AND PESTLE
Maple—natural finish

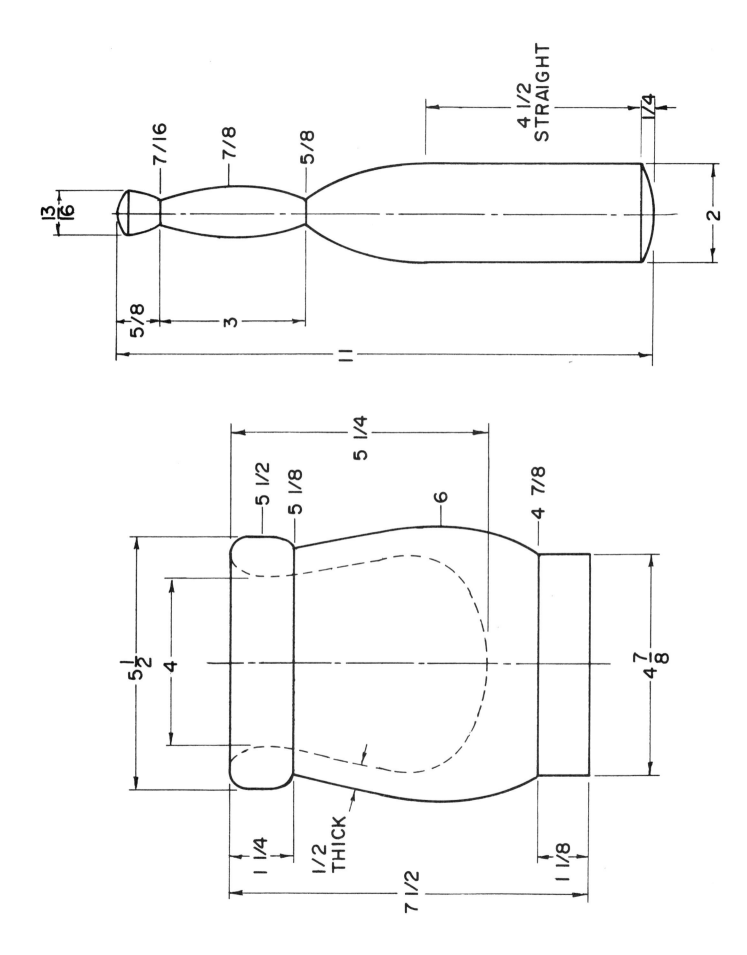

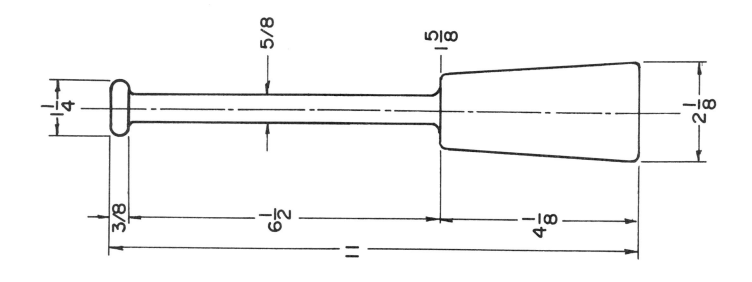
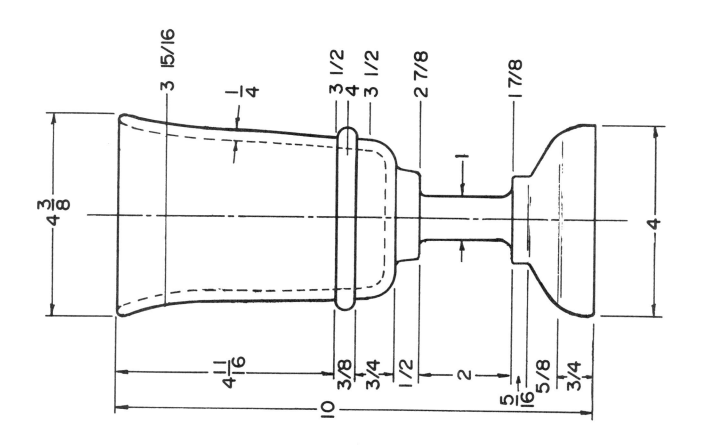

Candle Boxes

These boxes were usually wall-hanging. The first candle box is an unusual shelf candle box with a sliding top. The original was in old blue paint.

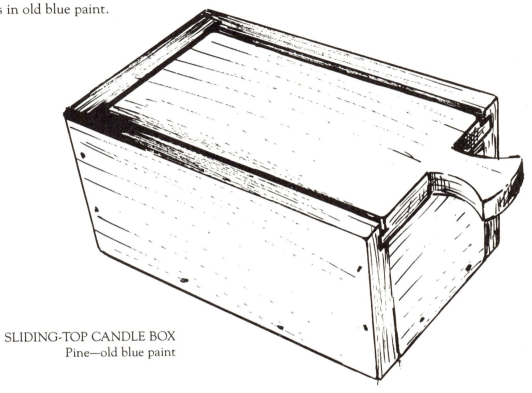

SLIDING-TOP CANDLE BOX
Pine—old blue paint

CANDLE BOX—VALLEY FORGE—c 1775
Cherry—rabbet joints, natural finish

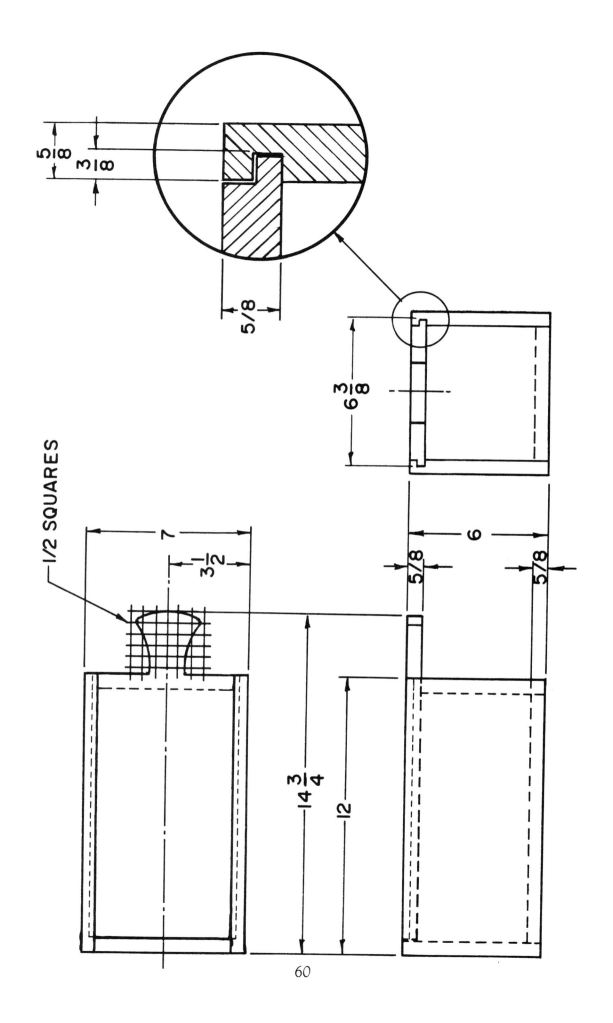

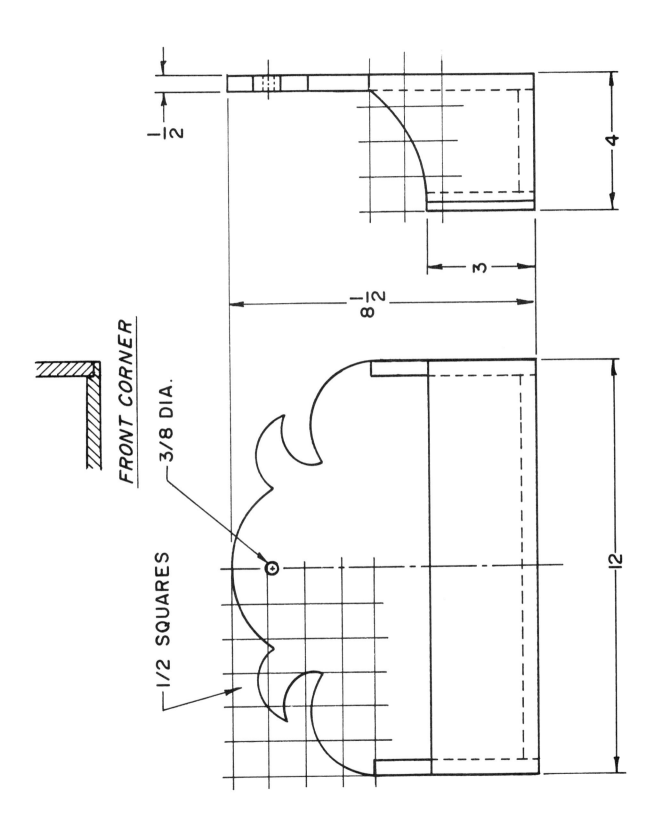

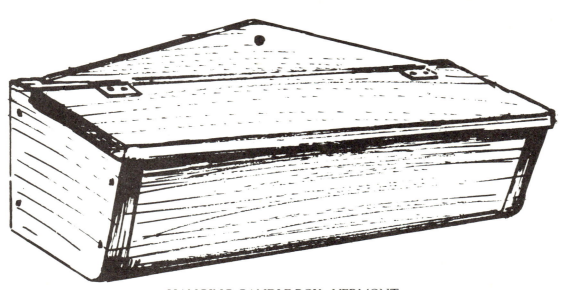

HANGING CANDLE BOX—VERMONT
Pine—old mustard paint

HANGING CANDLE BOX
Walnut—natural finish

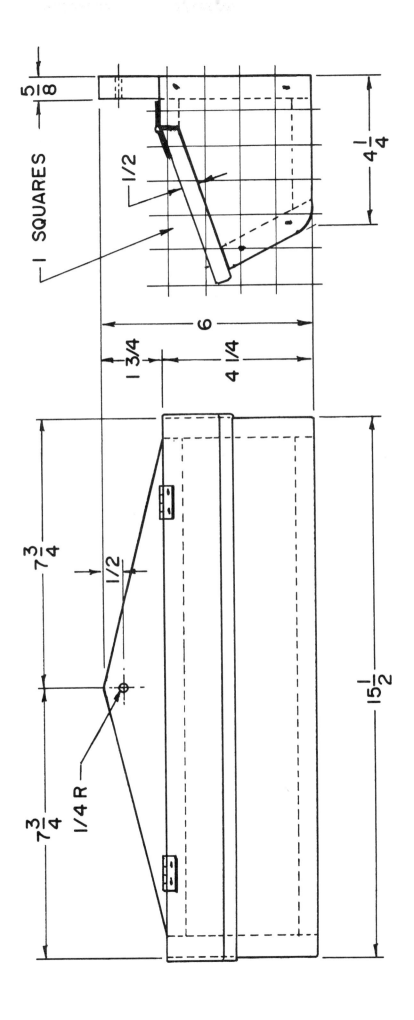

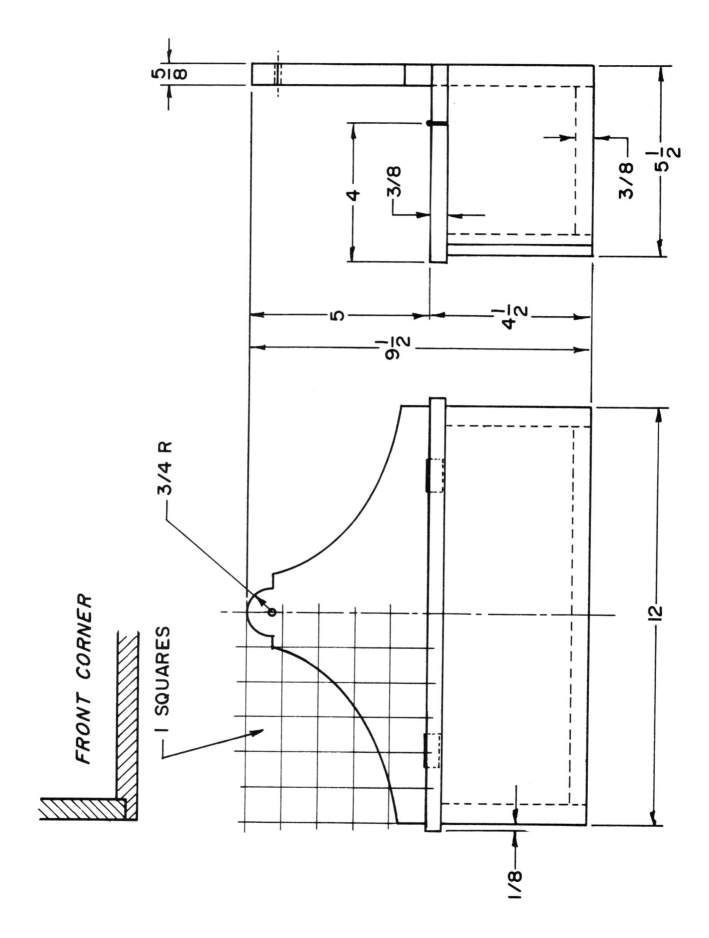

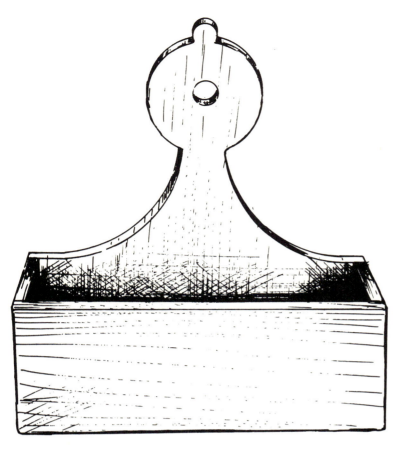

HANGING WALL BOX—c 1780
Pine—old gray paint

WALL BOX—NEW HAMPSHIRE
Pine—red paint

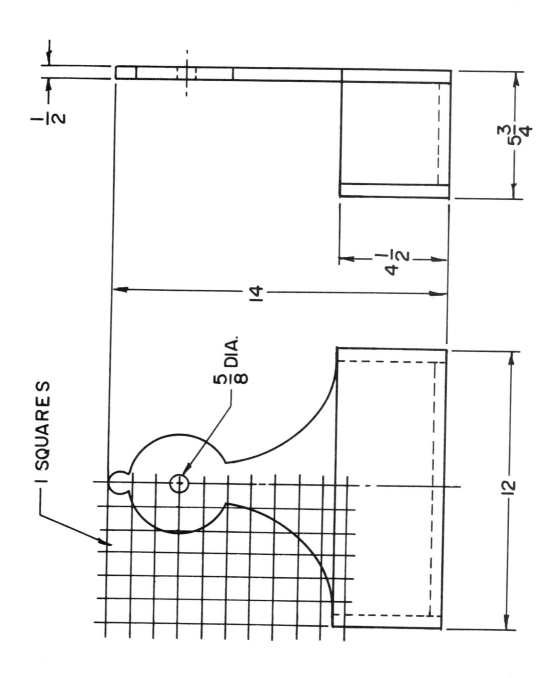

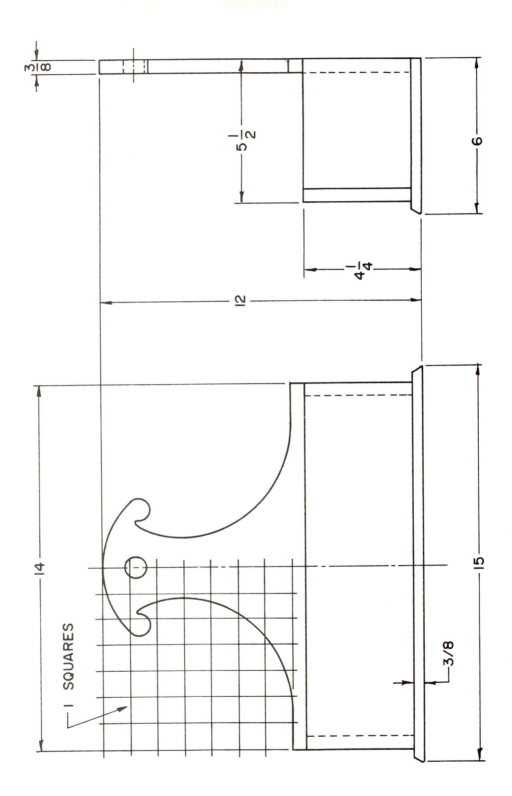

Utility Boxes

The utility boxes of yesterday were usually one of a kind and came in many shapes and sizes. They were usually made of pine and for a particular function.

UTILITY BOX WITH DOVETAIL CORNERS—c 1800
Pine—red paint

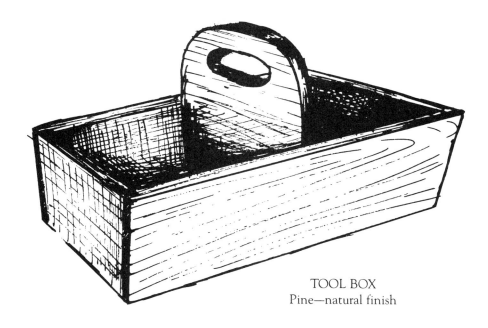

TOOL BOX
Pine—natural finish

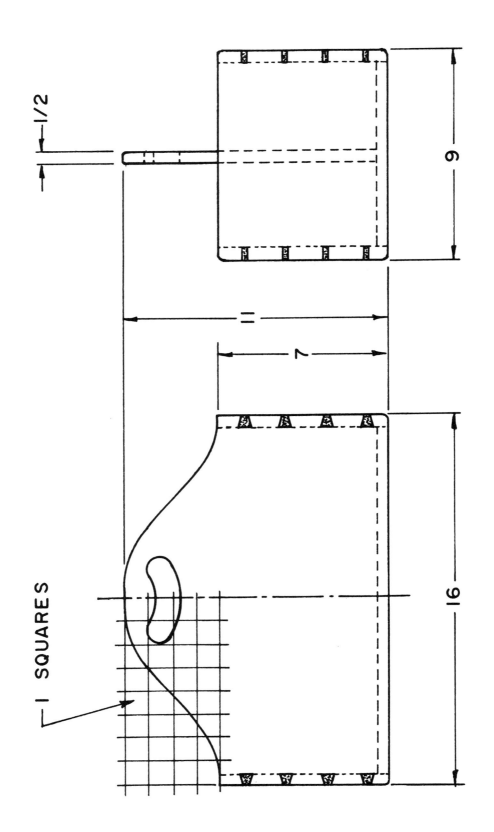

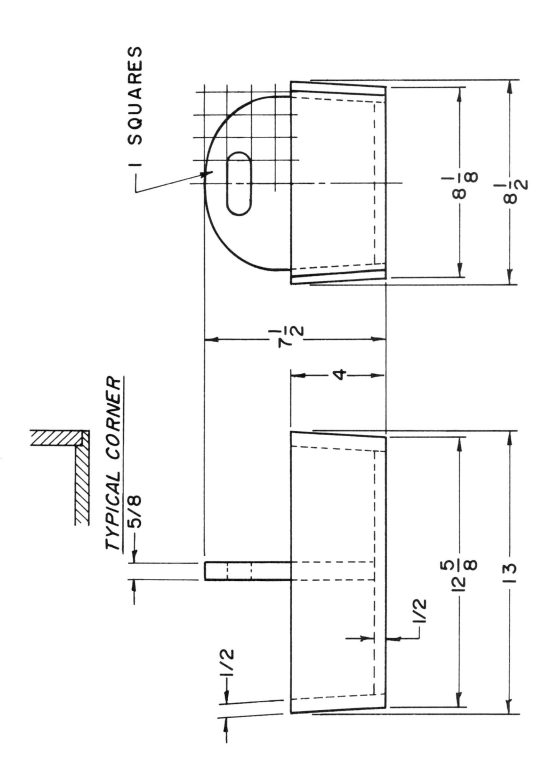

Knife Boxes

Also found in many various shapes and sizes, knife boxes were usually made of hardwood such as cherry, walnut, or mahogany. This knife box is splayed, scrolled, and dovetailed. It was made in New Hampshire around 1750 or so.

KNIFE TRAY—NEW ENGLAND—c 1750
Mahogany—natural finish

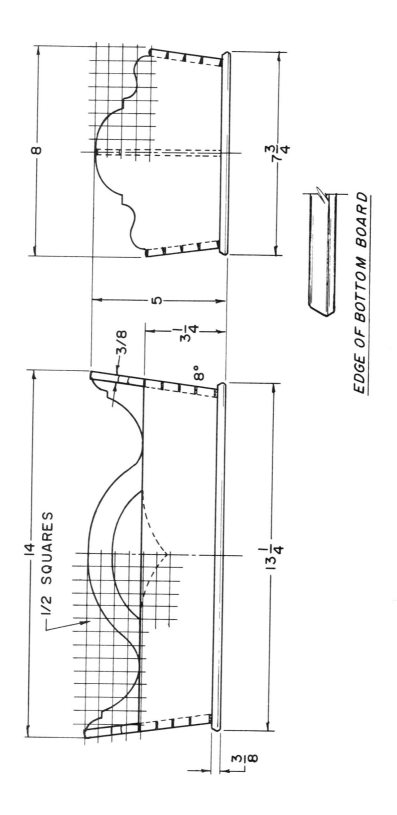

Candle Holder

This primitive wall candle holder is an early Shaker piece. The original was painted gray.

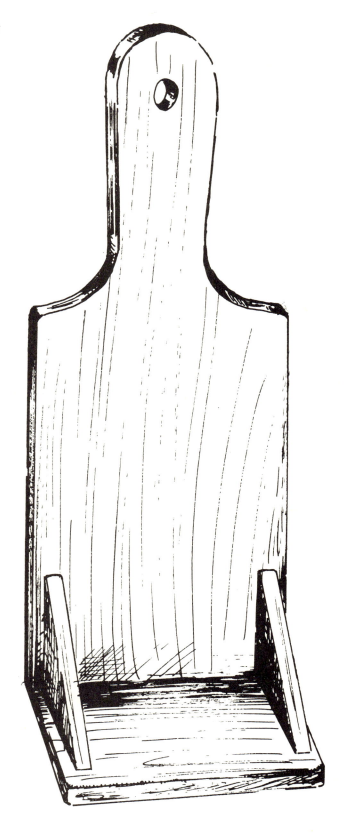

SHAKER CANDLE HOLDER
Pine—gray paint

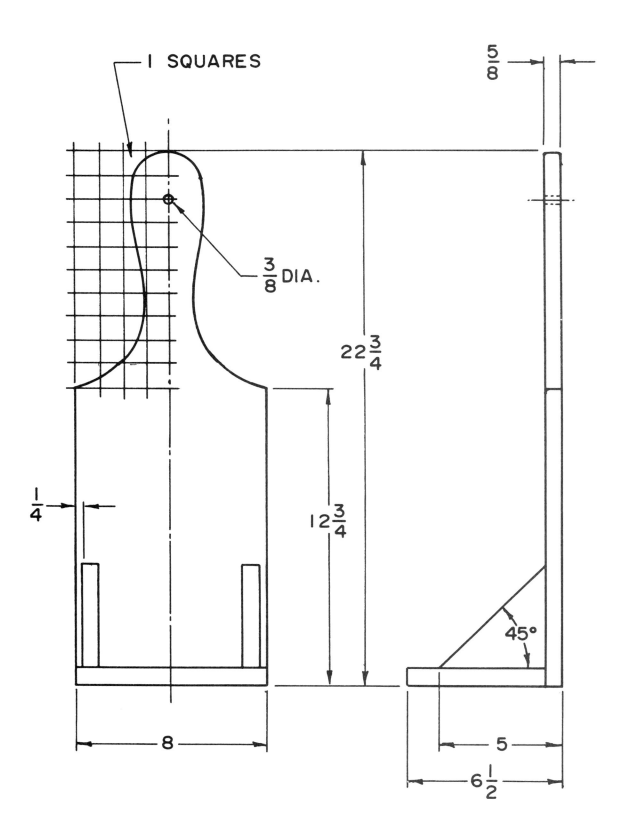

Desk Boxes

These were built similar to large blanket chests and were used to store many things from jewelry to toys. Desk boxes with locks sometimes contained, not valuable jewelry, but the family Bible. Many date back to 1675 or so. Some are divided into partitions or pigeonholes.

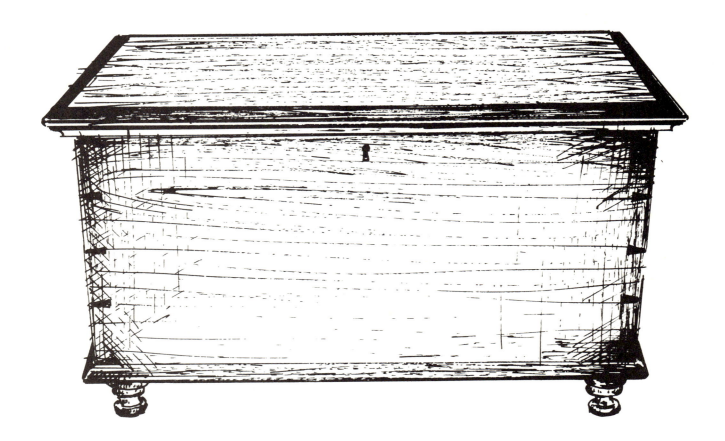

MINIATURE DESK BOX
Dovetail joints
Pine—old blue paint

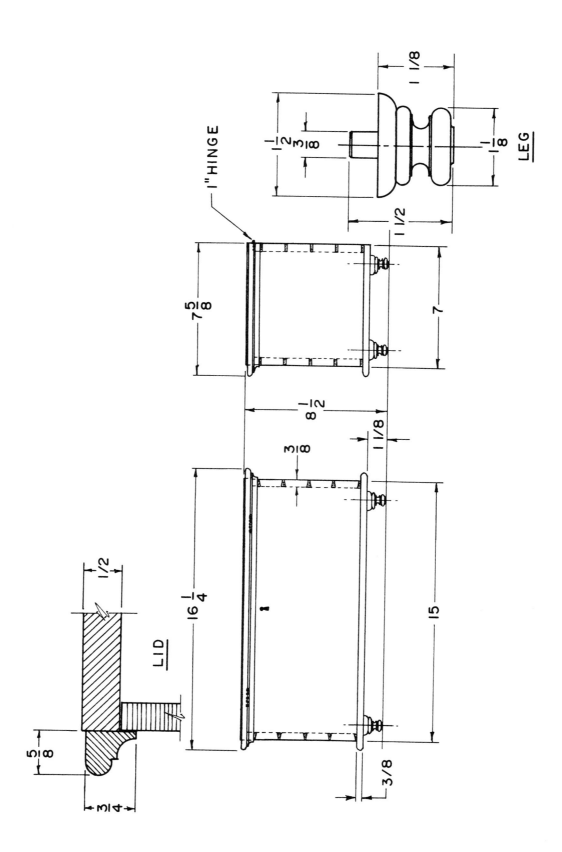

MINIATURE DESK BOX—PENNSYLVANIA
Snipe hinges—butt joints
Mahogany—light green paint

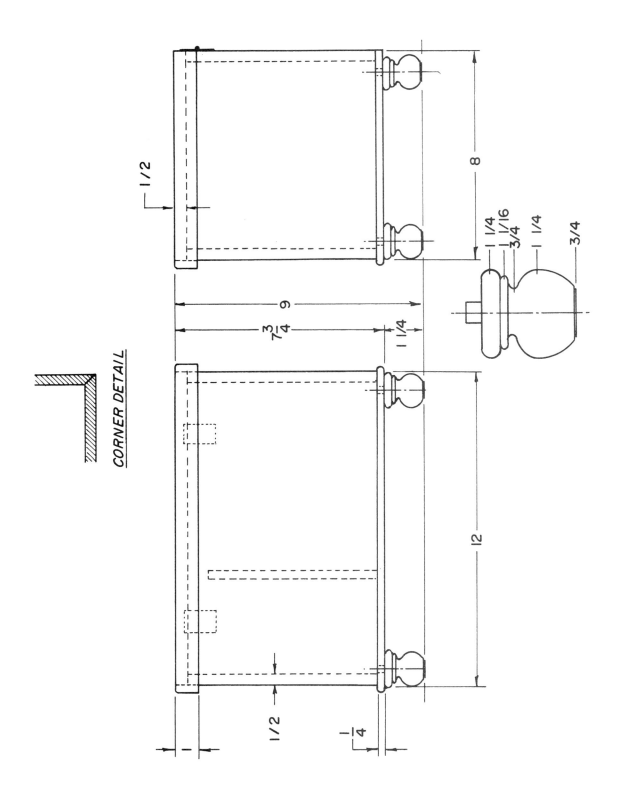

MINIATURE DESK BOX—c 1820
Pine—natural finish
Butt joints

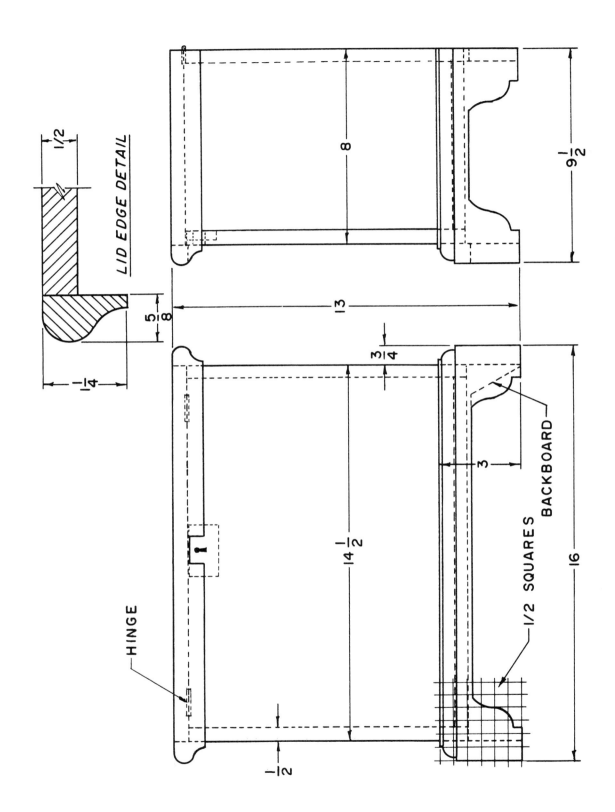

Blueberry Scoops

Usually homemade, these scoops were similar to the cranberry scoop, except not as wide. Today they make nice magazine racks.

BLUEBERRY SCOOP
Maple—natural finish

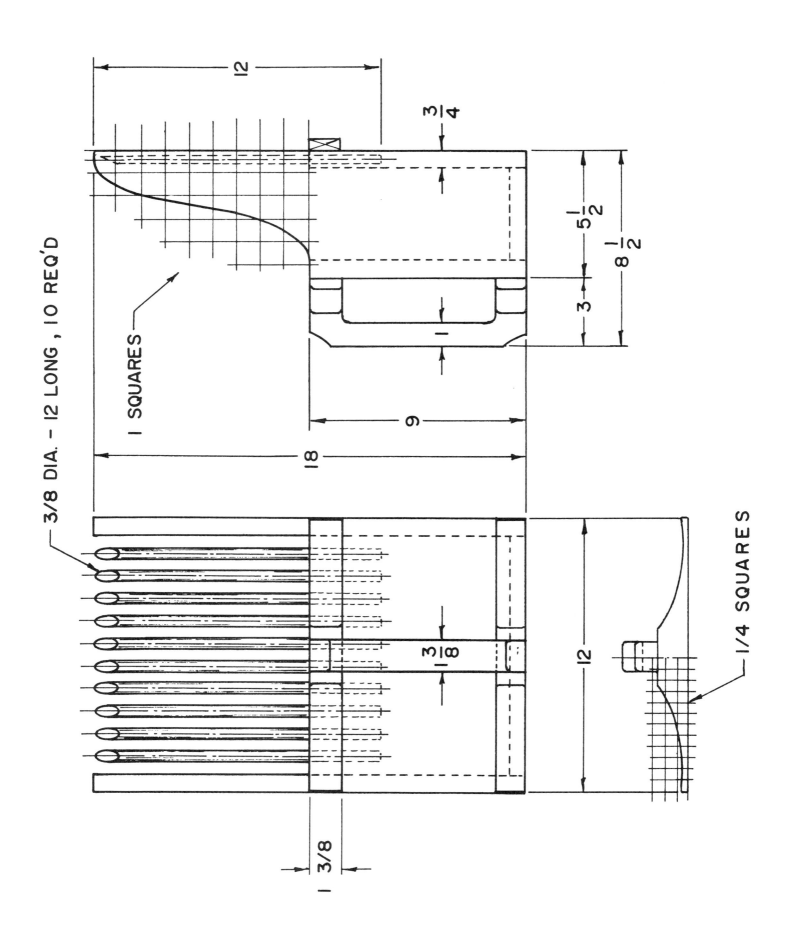

Part III

Antique Wall Projects

Early craftsmen made all kinds of wall boxes; large, small, with shelves, with drawers, some plain, some very decorative. As its name implies, a wall box is an object designed to hang from a nail on the wall. It was used to hold clay pipes, tobacco, spices, candles, and whatever else the housewife chose to put in it. In its simplest form, it was just a box without a lid. Later years brought lids, drawers, and shelves. No two were ever made alike and some were exceedingly beautiful.

Today with our modern kitchens with built-in shelves, it is hard to appreciate just how important and useful these old wall boxes must have been. As years went by, more and more drawers were added to the wall box until a nail or two would not support the wall box any longer and boxes of drawers were made to stand on other furniture or the floor.

Wall boxes used butt joints, rabbet joints, and dovetail joints and were held together by square nails. For that authentic look, be sure to add worn and rounded edges and corners to your new "antique."

Pipe and Tobacco Boxes

These boxes were used to store those long, white clay pipes of yesterday. The drawer at the bottom was used to store tobacco. These were somewhat formal and were usually made of mahogany or walnut and sometimes of pine. It was not unusual for the heads of the square nails used in construction to be visible, with no effort to hide them.

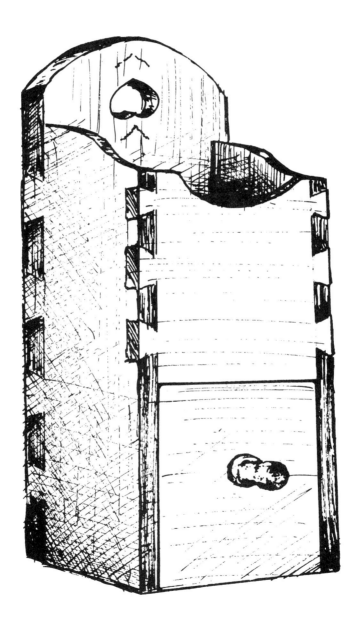

PIPE AND TOBACCO BOX—CAPE COD
Dovetail joints
Walnut—natural finish

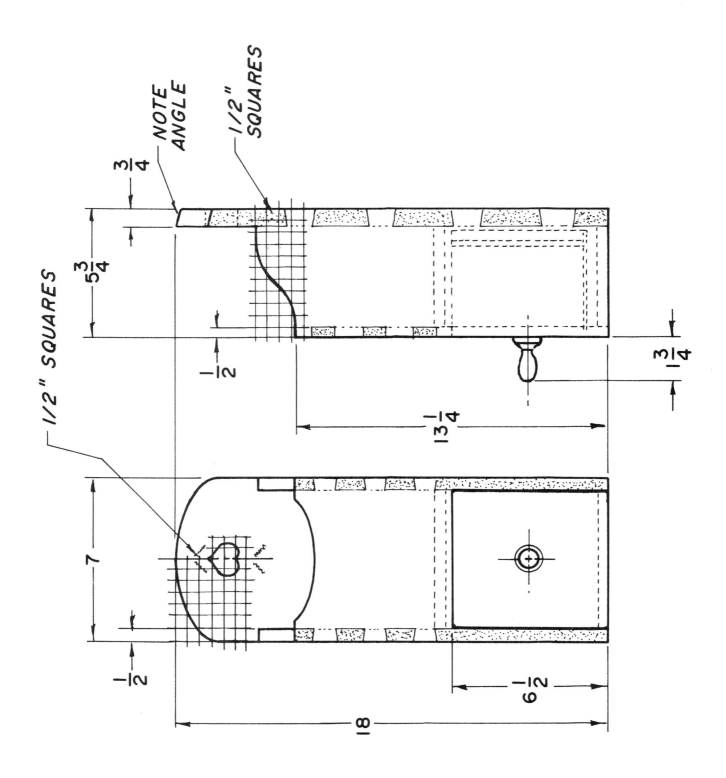

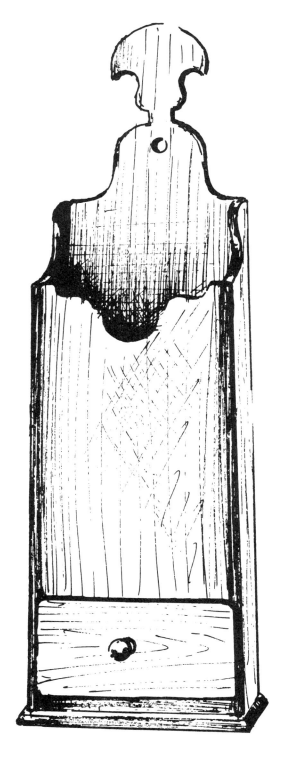

PIPE AND TOBACCO BOX—c 1775
Mahogany—natural finish

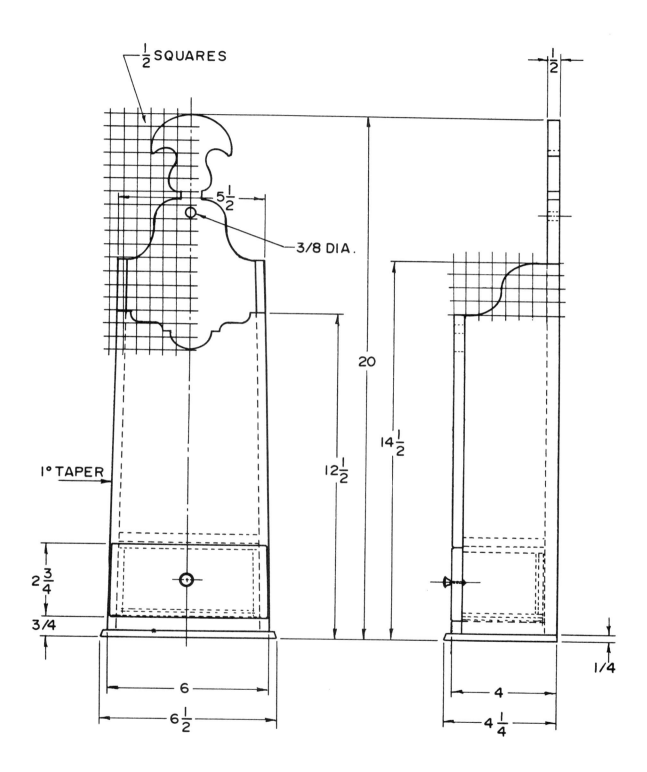

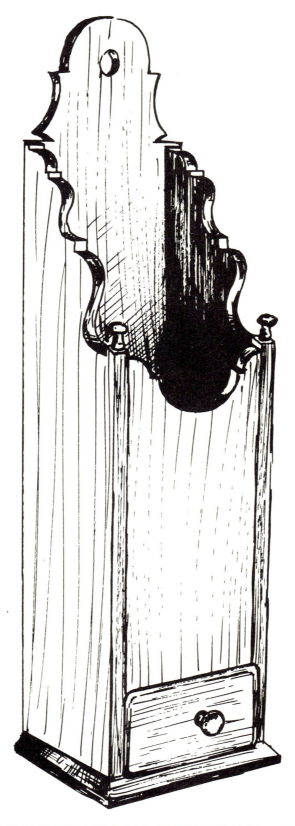

PIPE AND TOBACCO BOX—NEW ENGLAND—c 1780
Pine and chestnut—brown paint

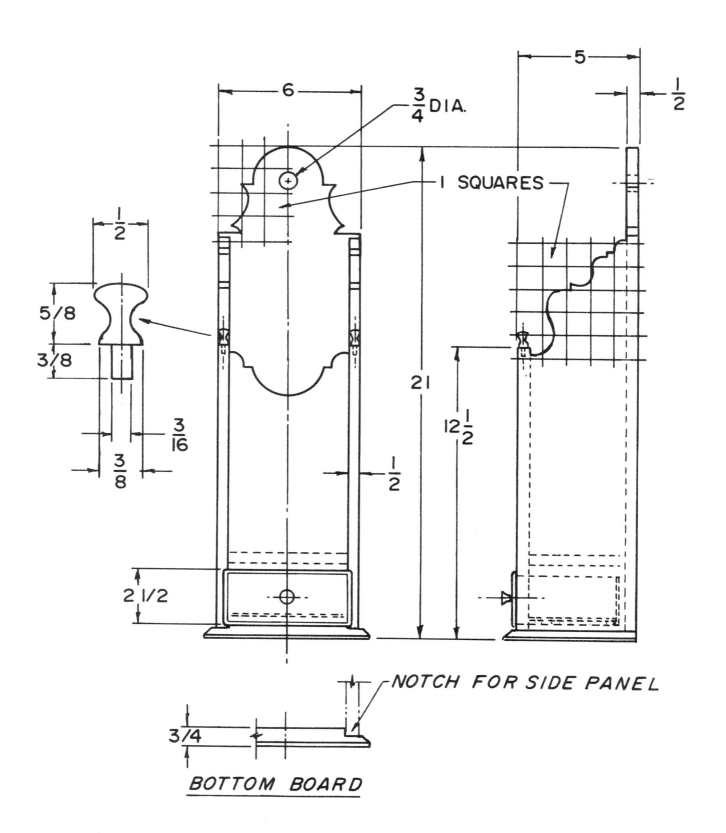

Wall Boxes

Extremely useful today, wall boxes add that extra charm to any Colonial setting. Some are painted; others are left clear. Don't be afraid to leave the heads of the square nails showing.

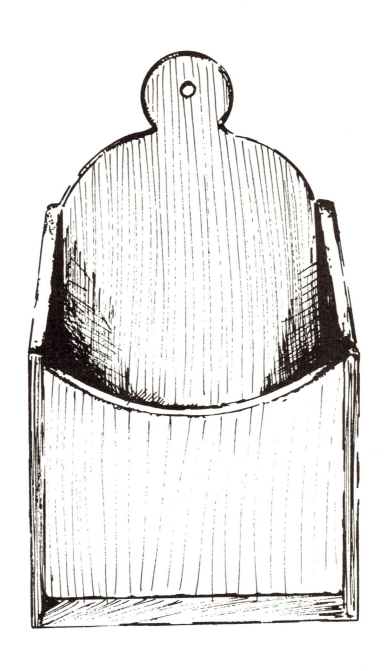

HANGING WALL BOX—c 1850
Pine—old blue paint

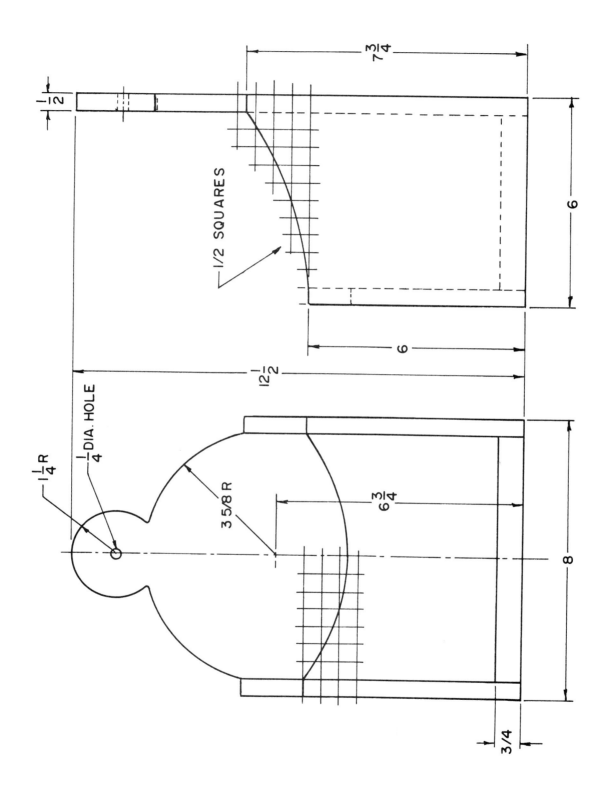

HANGING WALL BOX
Pine—natural finish

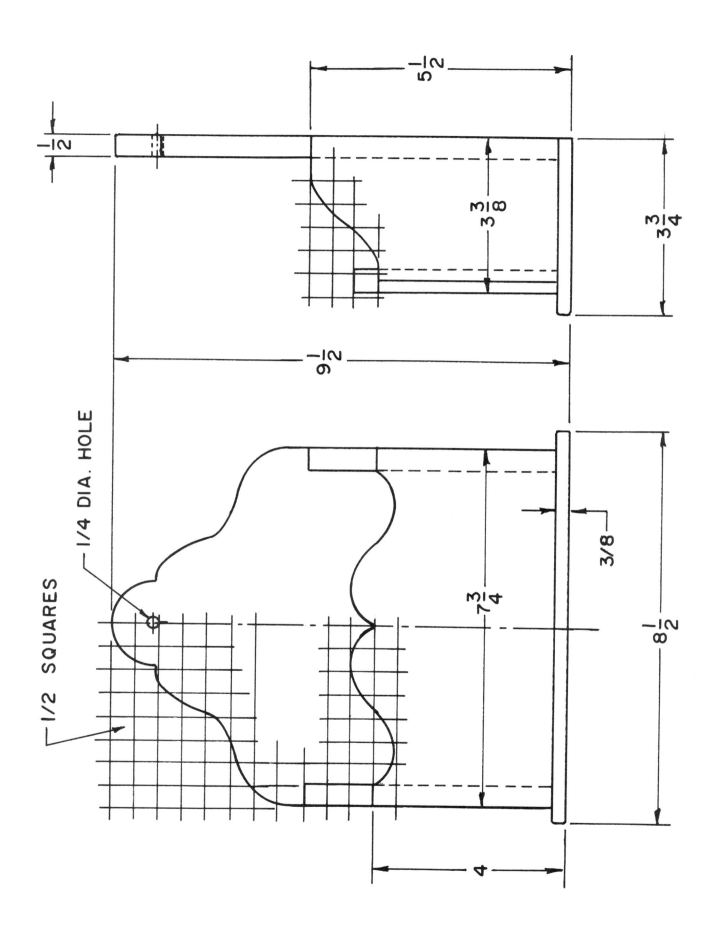

Hanging Shelves

These were made to fit a particular need in a particular room or space. Some were very plain; others had shelves with dividers that led later to drawers. Some fit along walls, while others were built to fit into a corner. Today, these wonderful old shelves can be used to display a variety of things.

HANGING SHELF—c 1810
Pine—red and blue paint

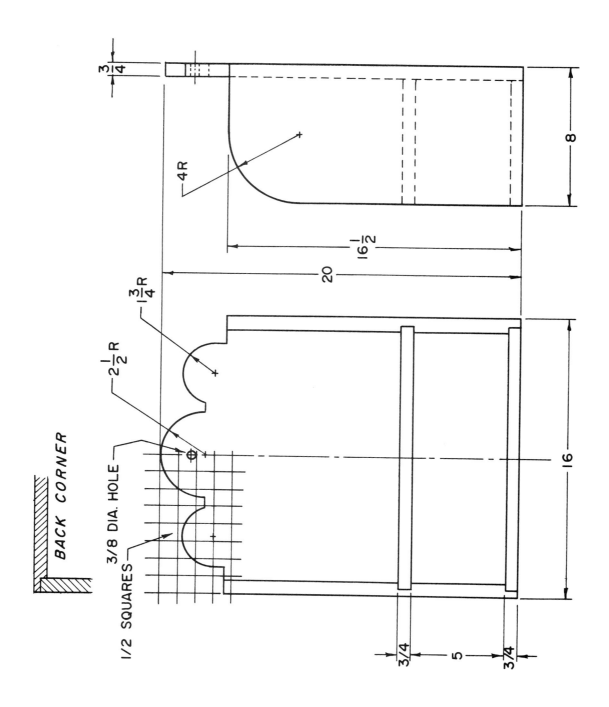

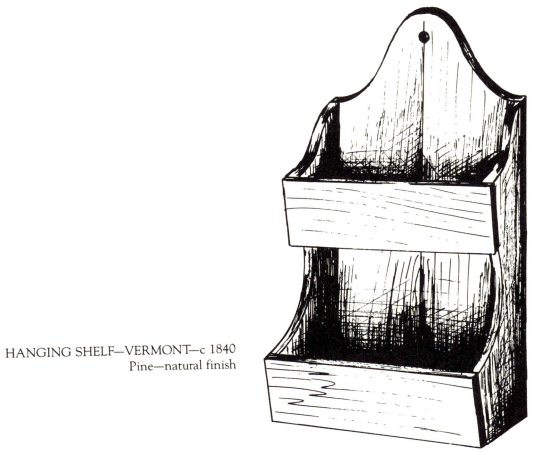

HANGING SHELF—VERMONT—c 1840
Pine—natural finish

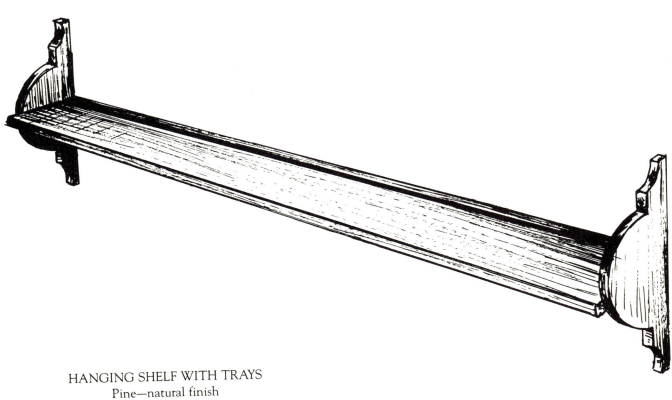

HANGING SHELF WITH TRAYS
Pine—natural finish

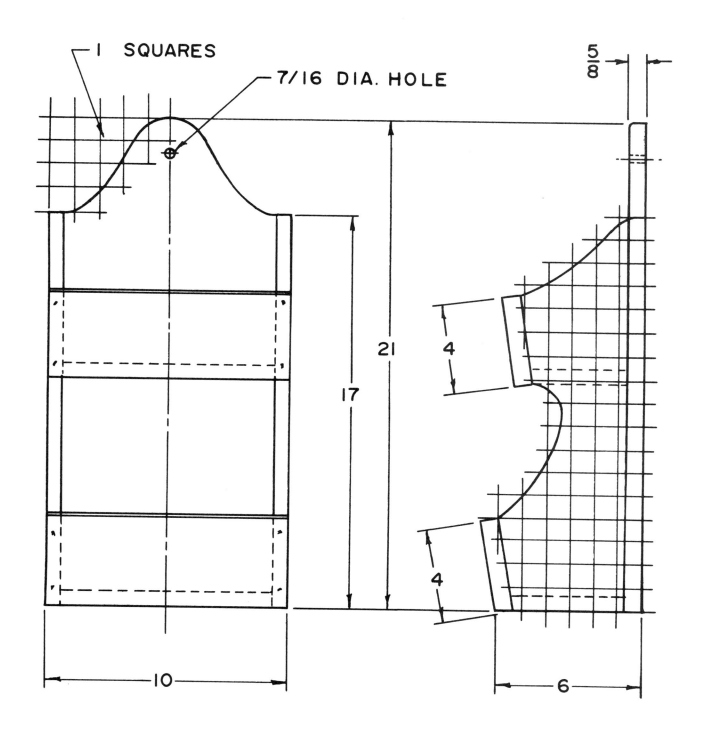

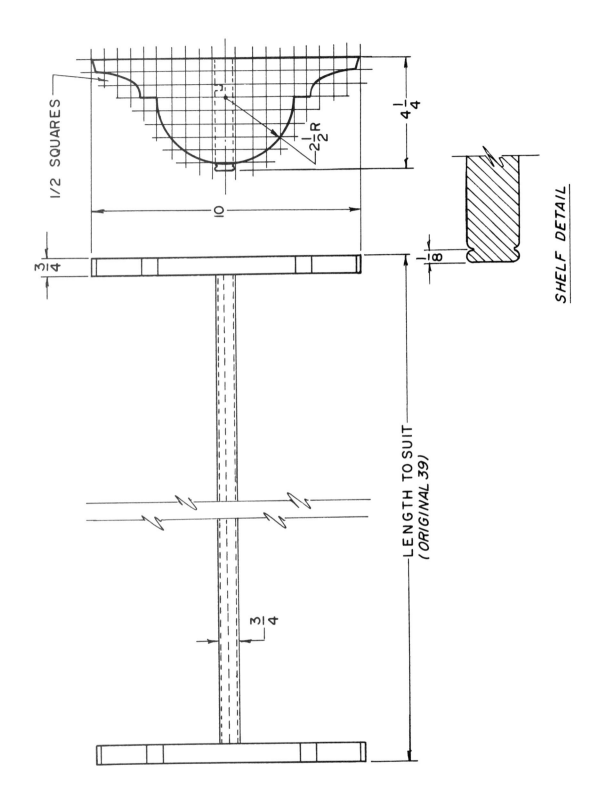

HANGING SHELVES
Pine—natural finish

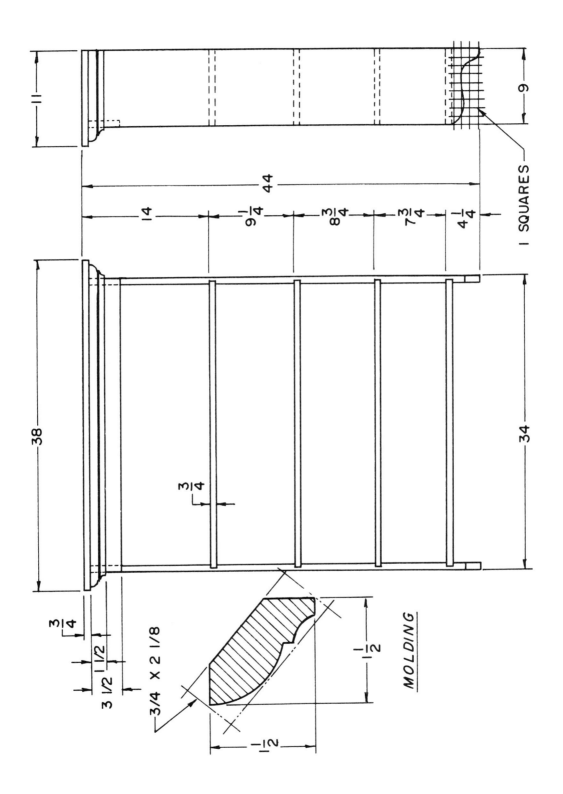

HANGING WALL SHELF—NEW HAMPSHIRE—c 1835
Birch—natural finish

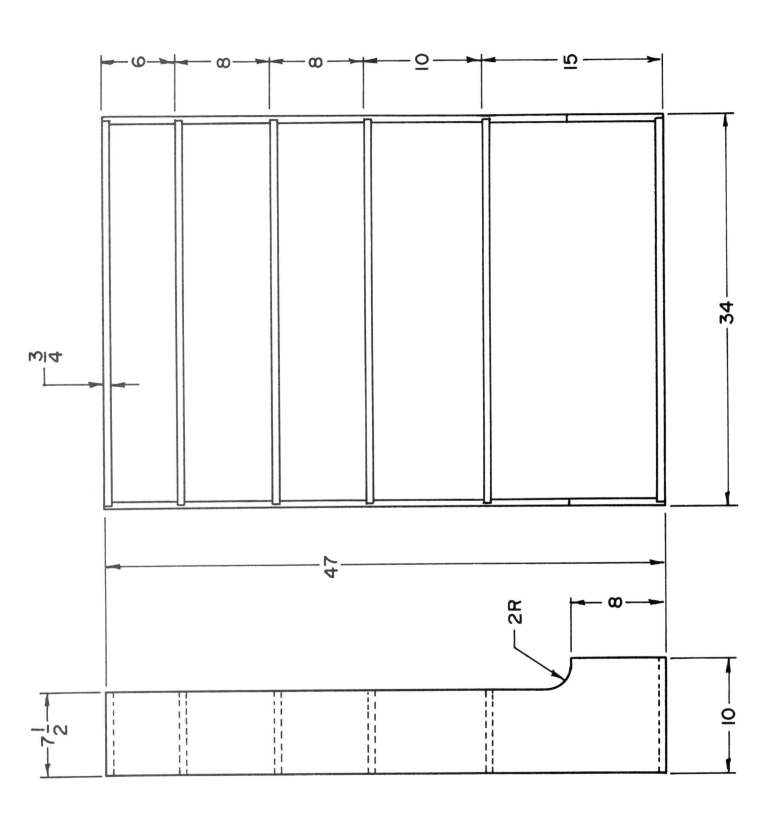

HANGING WALL SHELF—NEW HAMPSHIRE
Maple—natural finish

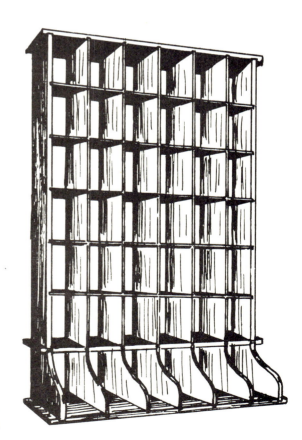

POST OFFICE SORTING BOX
Maple—natural finish

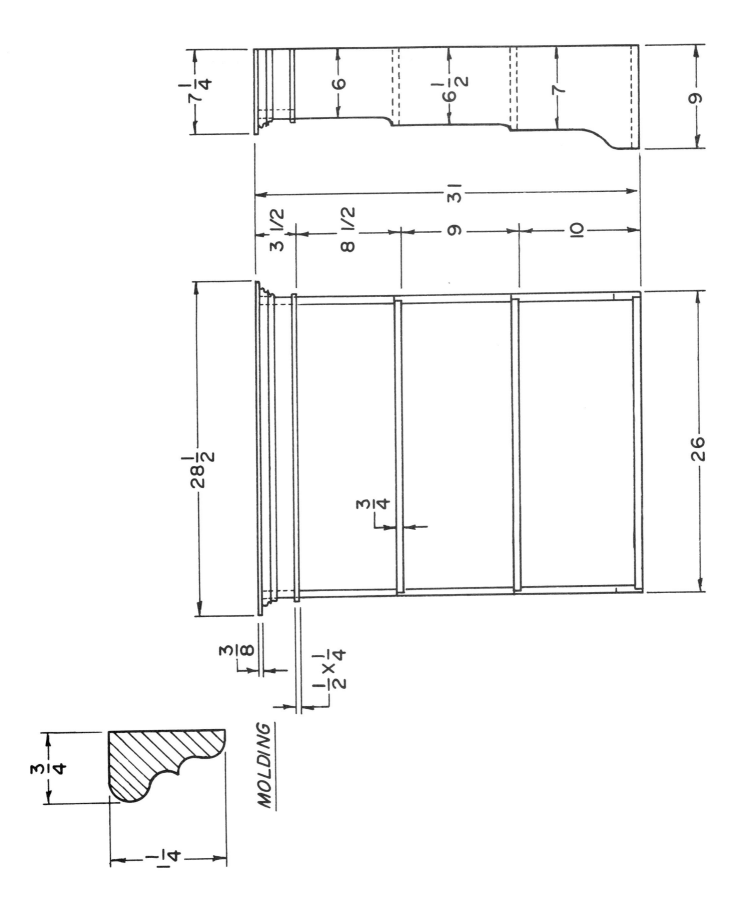

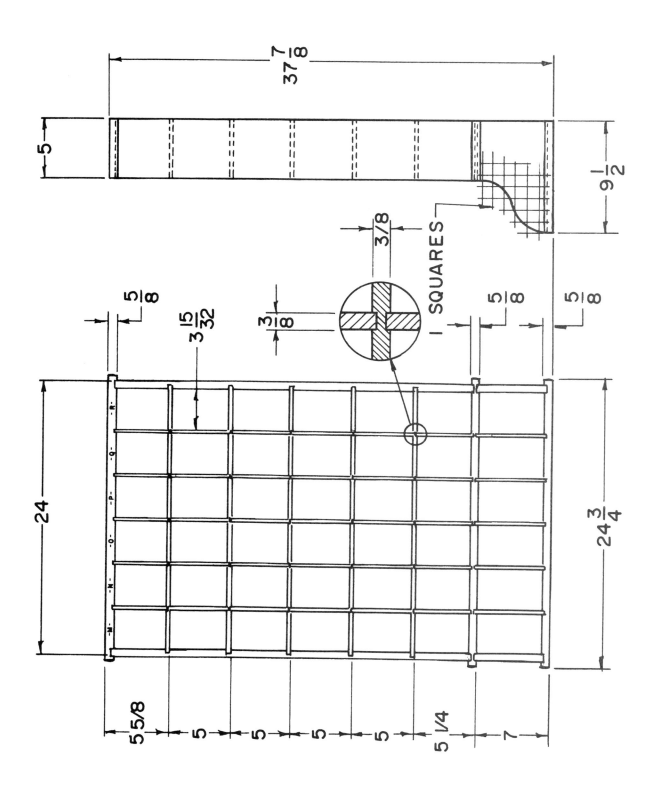

CORNER HANGING WALL SHELF
Pine—painted grain (brown over mustard paint)

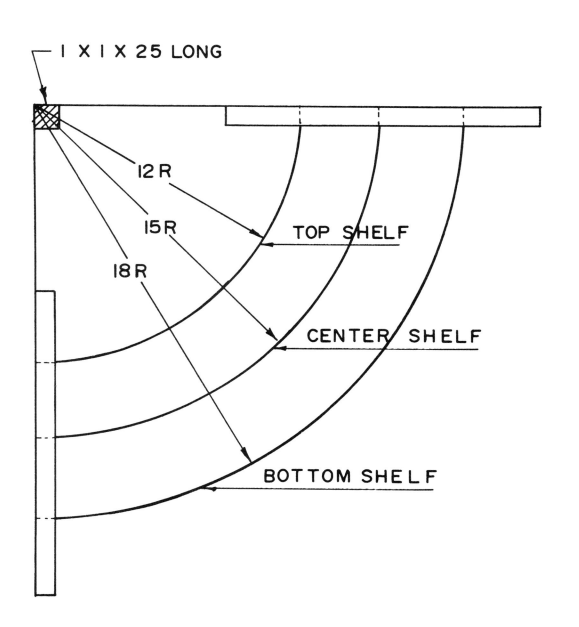

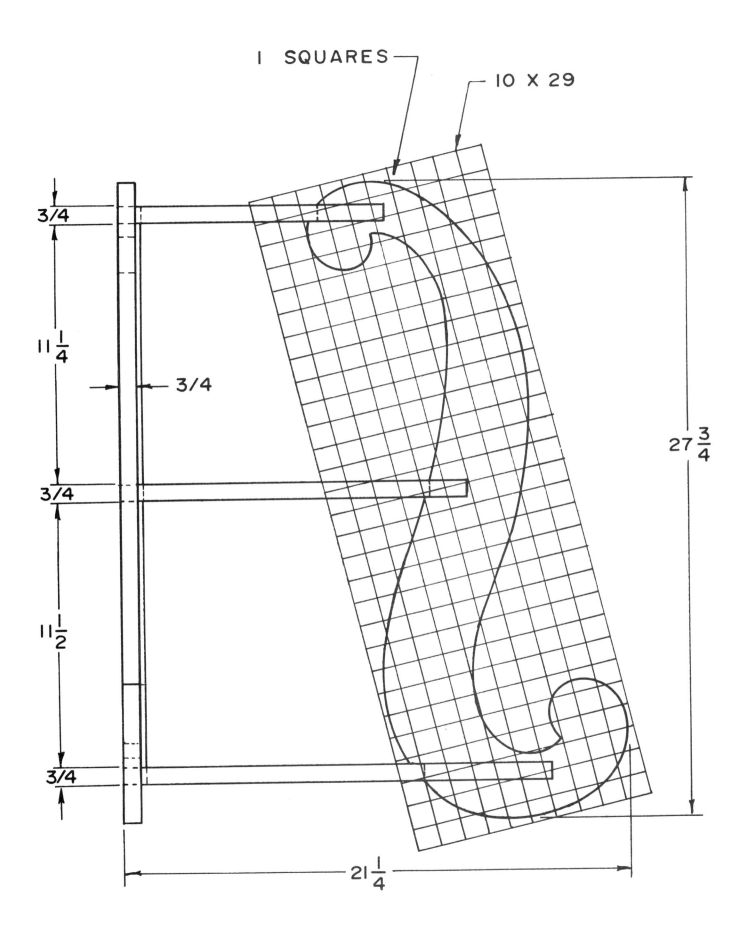

SHAKER TWO-DRAWER SHELF—c 1830
Cherry and pine—natural finish

FOUR-DRAWER HANGING SHELF
Pine—gray paint

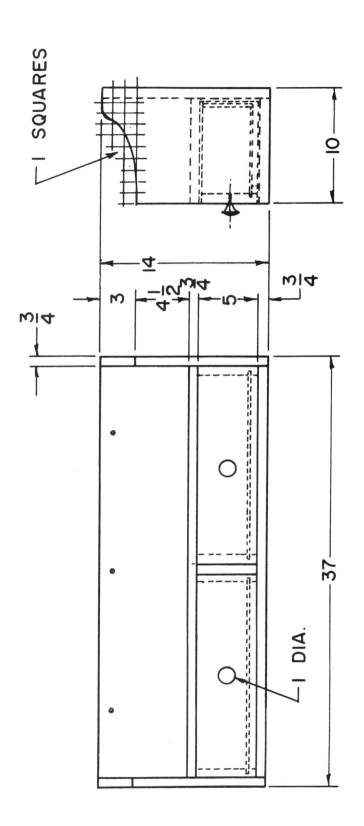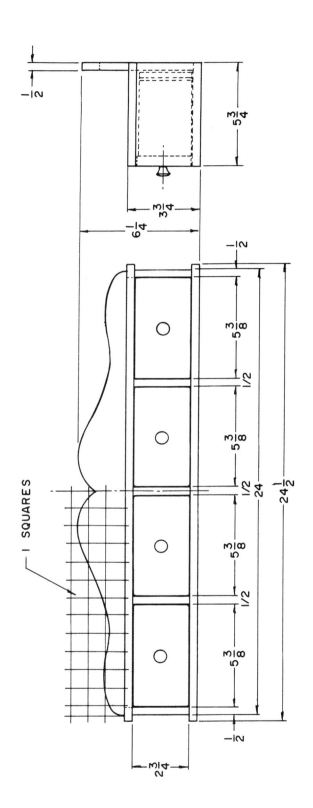

HANGING WALL BOX—LANCASTER COUNTY, PA.—c 1820
Spruce—natural finish with yellow, black, red letters

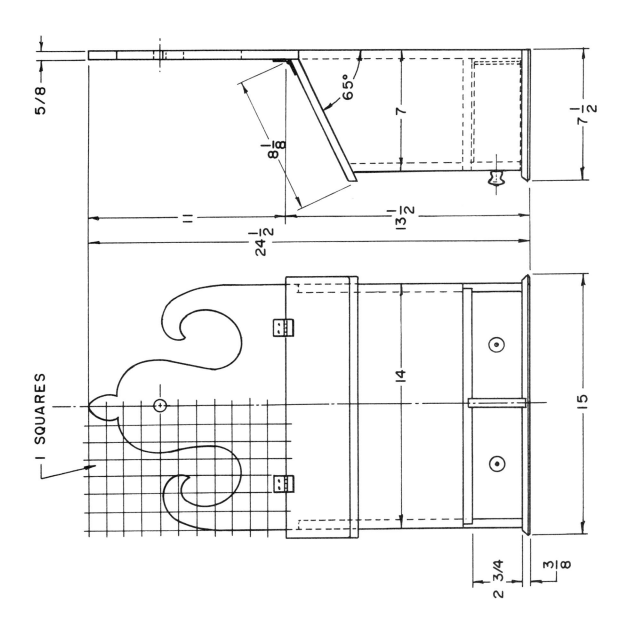

HANGING WALL BOX WITH GRADUATED DRAWERS
Pine—light blue paint—with square cut nails, wooden knobs

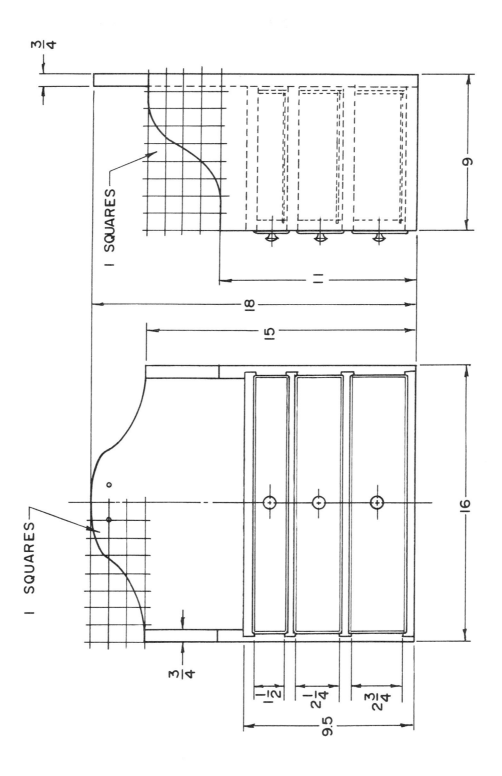

HANGING SHELF—CONNECTICUT
Pine—natural finish

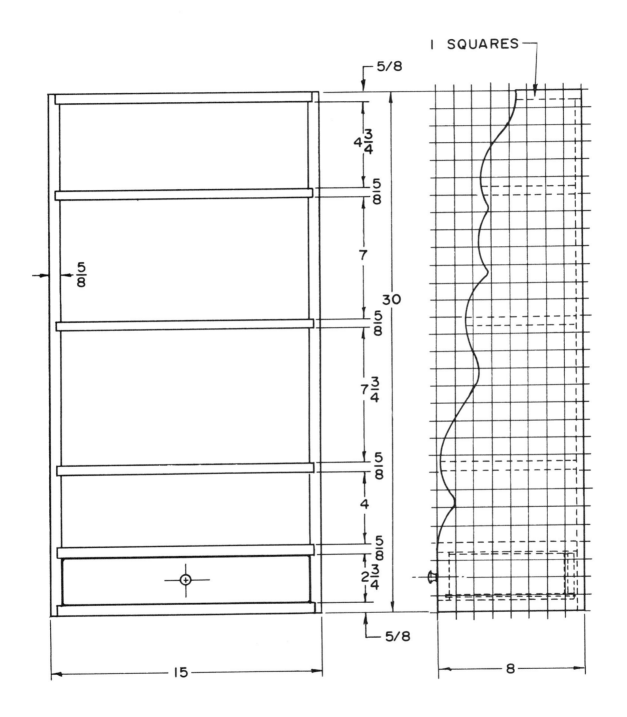

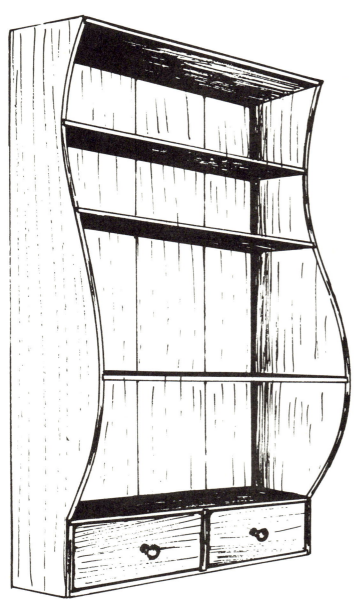

HANGING SHELF—VERMONT
Dovetail drawers
Pine—old blue paint inside shelves

HANGING SPICE BOX
Walnut—natural finish

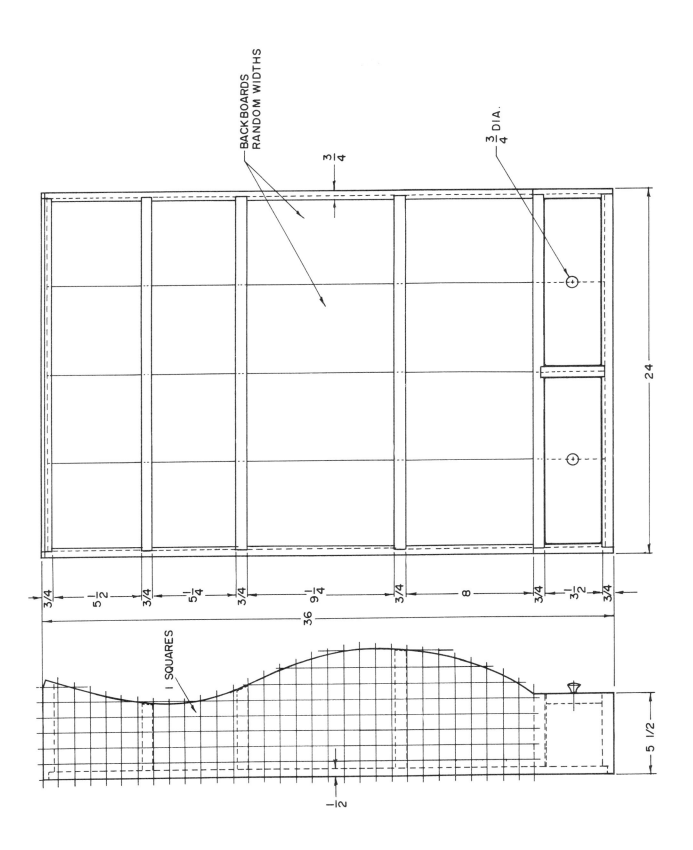

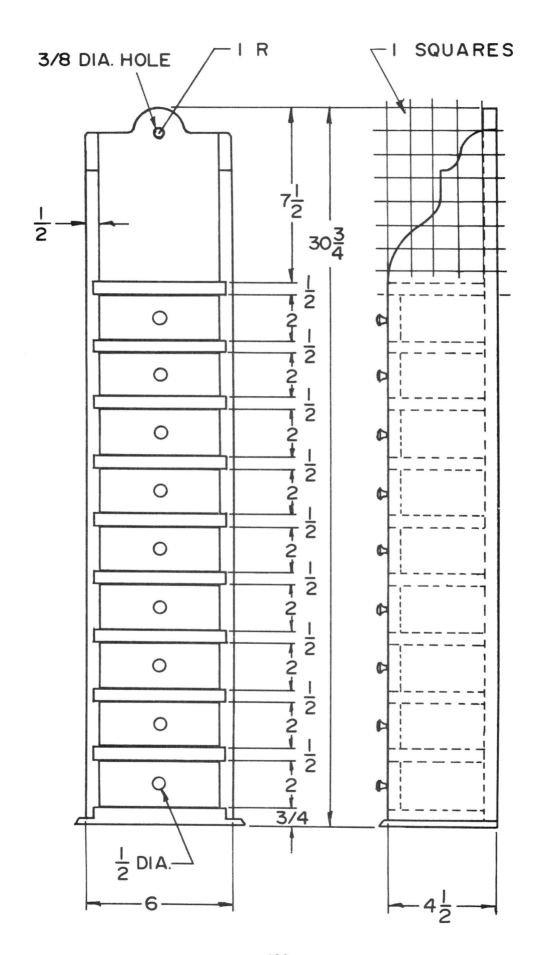

Spoon Racks

Spoon racks were used to display spoons only; forks were not known in Early America. Early spoons were made of pewter, and people were proud of their pewter spoons. This was their way to store and display them. Knives were very crude at that time and not made of pewter, thus were hidden away in the knife drawers below.

Spoon racks range from the very simple, made of pine, to the very elaborate, made of mahogany. Illustrated here are samples from each end of the spectrum.

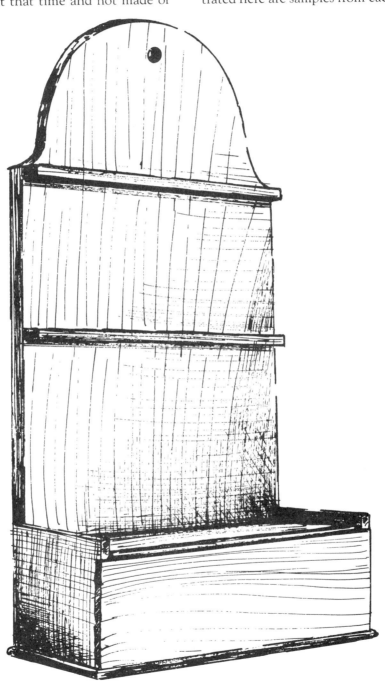

SPOON RACK WITH CANDLE BOX—c 1765
Cherry—old blue-gray paint

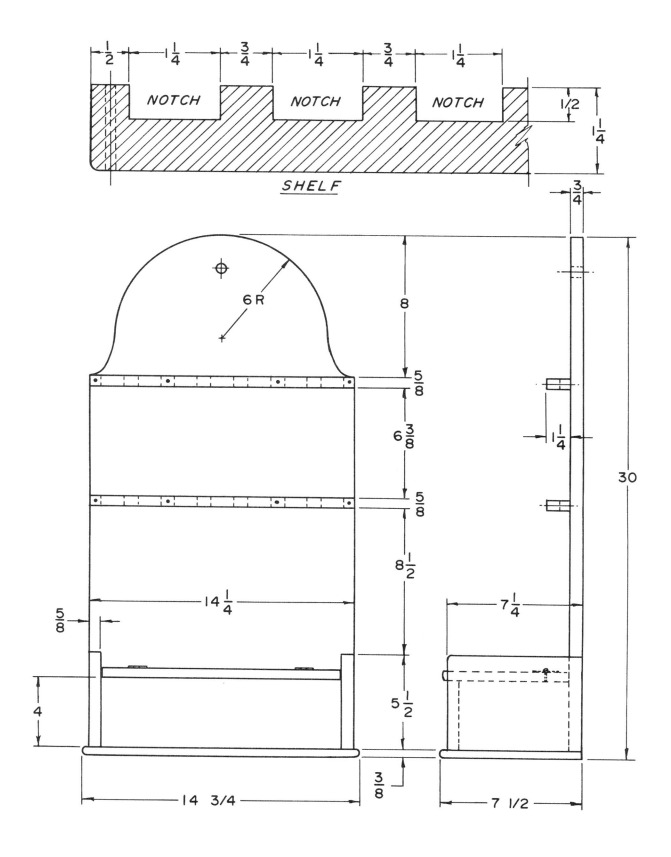

SPOON RACK WITH DRAWER
Pine—natural finish

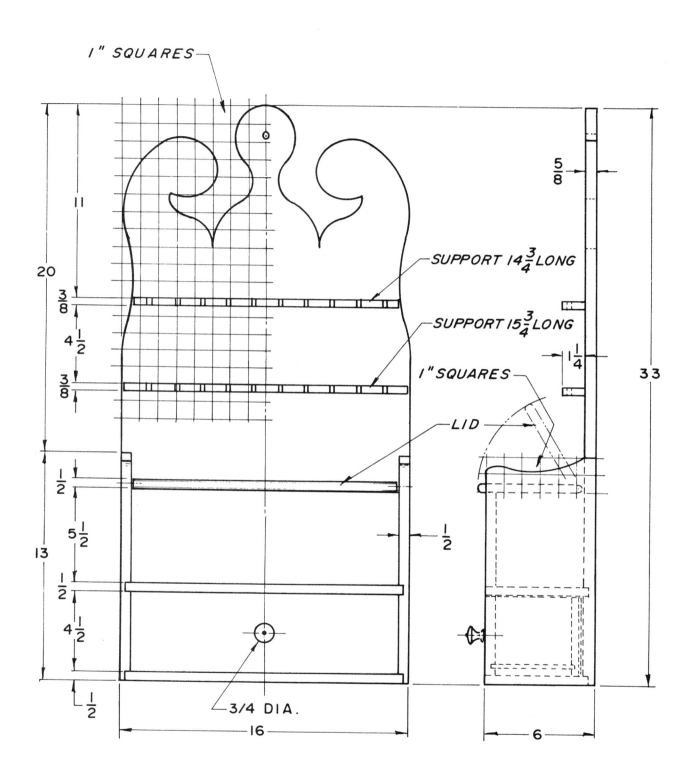

SPOON RACK WITH DRAWER
Cherry—natural finish

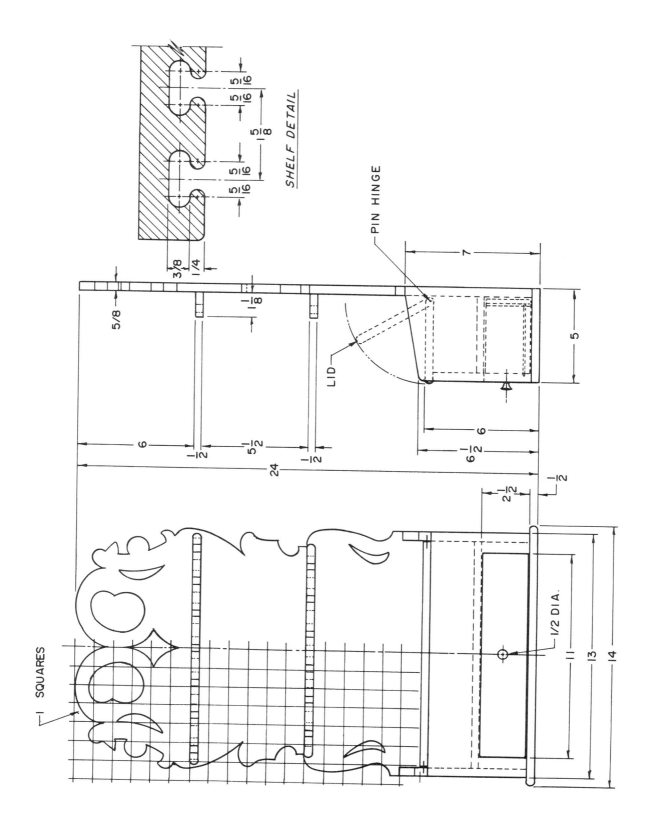

Mirrors

Mirror glass was extremely rare and expensive in Colonial days. Up to 1750 or so, most people who wanted to see themselves had to gaze into a water bucket. Because of the high cost of glass, early mirrors were made very small. This example measured only 8 3/8 inches overall. It is made of mahogany and very plain.

SMALL QUEEN ANNE MIRROR—NEW ENGLAND—c 1725
Mahogany—natural finish

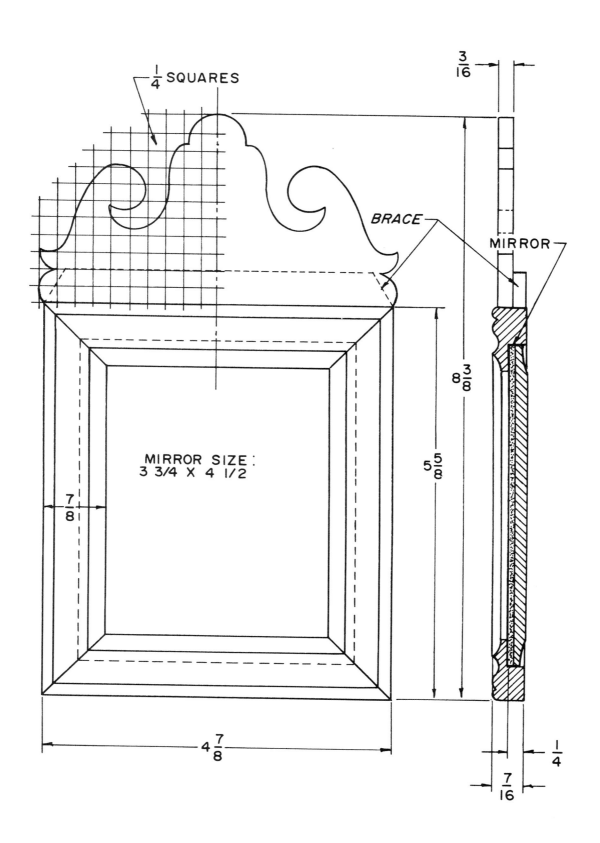

Wall Cupboards

Similar to hanging shelves, wall cupboards were also a necessity of life due to the lack of built-ins.

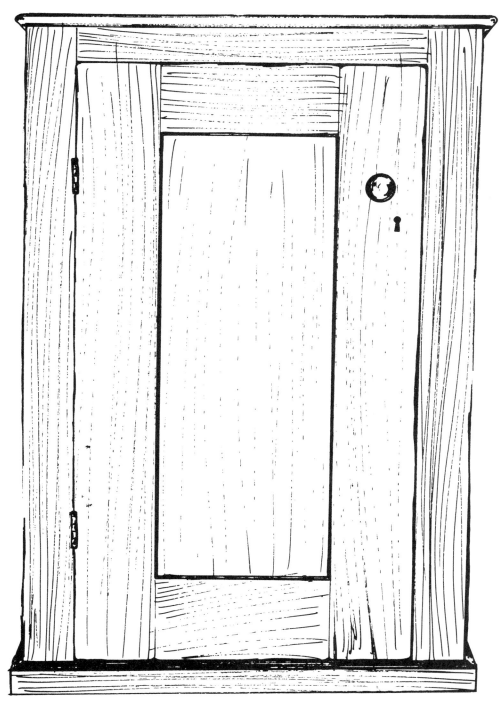

HANGING SHAKER CUPBOARD—NEW HAMPSHIRE
Pine—olive green paint

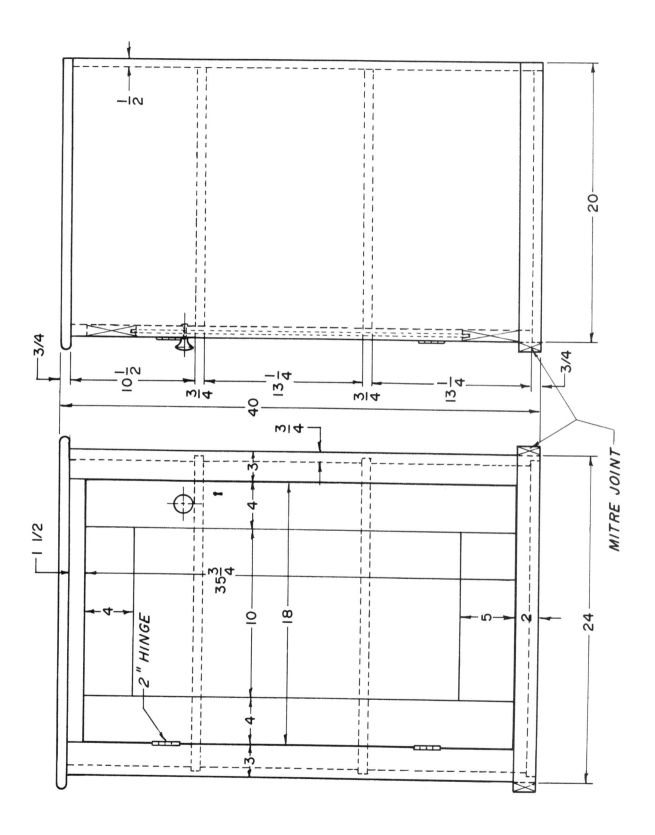

HANGING CUPBOARD WITH BRASS HARDWARE—c 1790
Walnut—natural finish

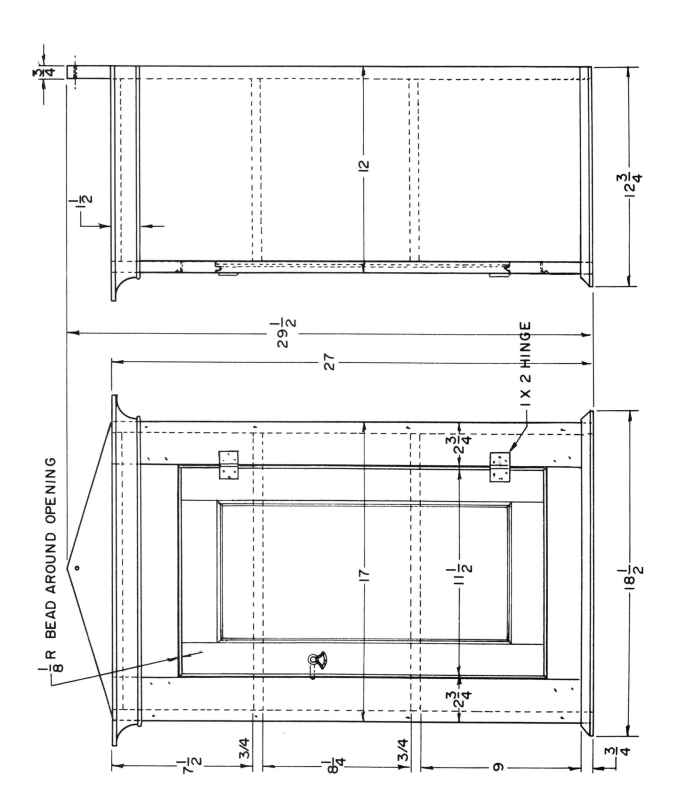

Apothecary Chests

These chests were used to store various drugs used in years past. Today they make a nice storage area for other things. Be sure to use ½-inch-diameter, white porcelain knobs.

APOTHECARY CHEST
Pine—natural finish

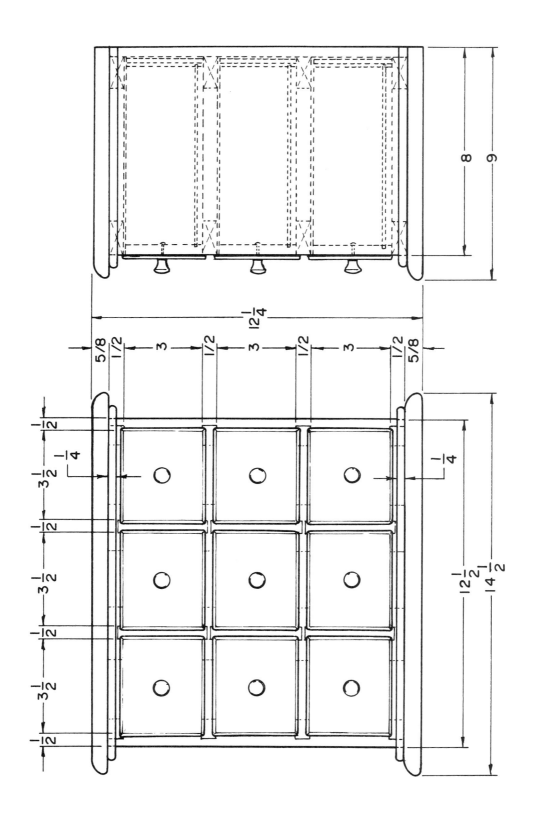

Coffin Clock

Sometimes referred to as a box-clock, the coffin clock adds warmth to any room. The original can be found in Old Sturbridge Village and was made by Aaron Willard, Jr. of Boston, Massachusetts, in 1820. It was made of Cuban mahogany and had an eight-day weight-driven movement with an alarm. An excellent eight-day spring movement with a 20¼-inch pendulum can be purchased from any of the clock supply houses listed in the Appendix. Be sure to note *depth* of the movement, as the original clock was very thin (4¼ inches). If necessary, increase this thickness to fit the available movement.

Although not authentic, quartz movements can be found that swing a 20¼-inch pendulum and are easy to install and run. After they are in place, no one can tell the difference.

A paper dial face can be purchased from any of the clock suppliers listed in the Appendix. Use a 7-inch-diameter dial such as Merritt's #R-700.

COFFIN CLOCK—c 1820
Cuban mahogany—natural finish

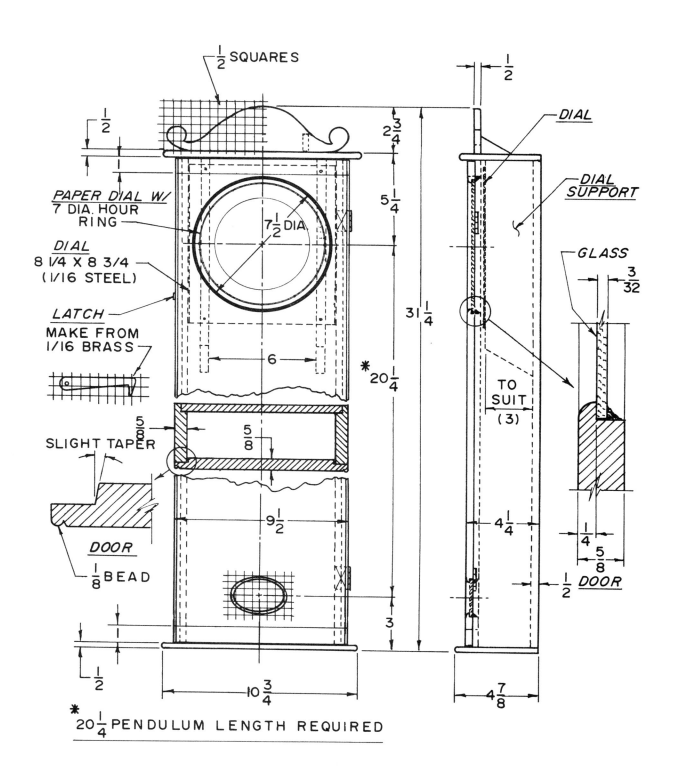

DIAL DETAIL

Part IV

Antique Floor Projects

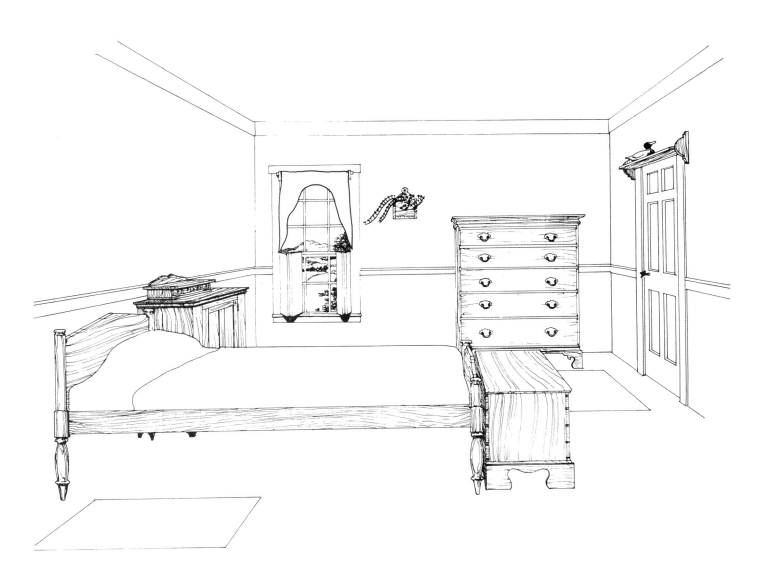

Stools and Benches

There are no two stools or benches alike. Each farmer or craftsman had his own idea of what a stool or bench should look like. A visit to an antique shop or museum will verify this fact. The very first stools were probably simple three-legged affairs with plain, bored tops. Later came solid legs with side boards to make them more stable. Stools and benches used simple butt joints nailed together with square-cut nails. Most were made of pine because it was lightweight, which made them easy to carry around. Chairs were later developed from the stool's basic design.

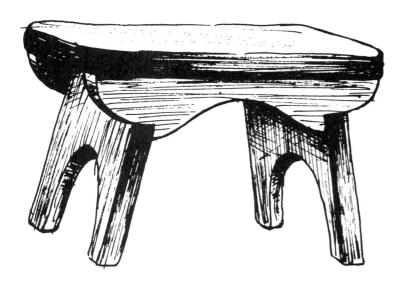

STOOL
Pine—brown paint

WIDE STOOL
Pine—natural finish

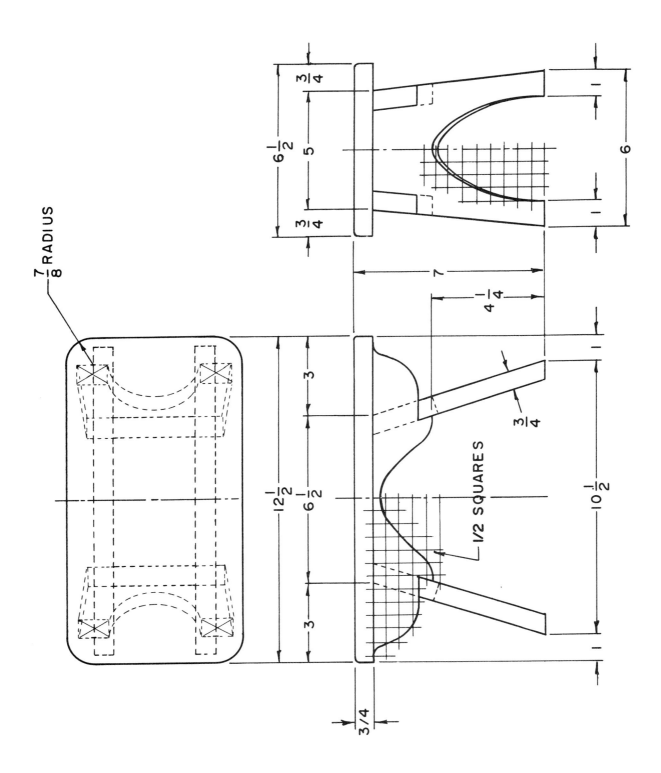

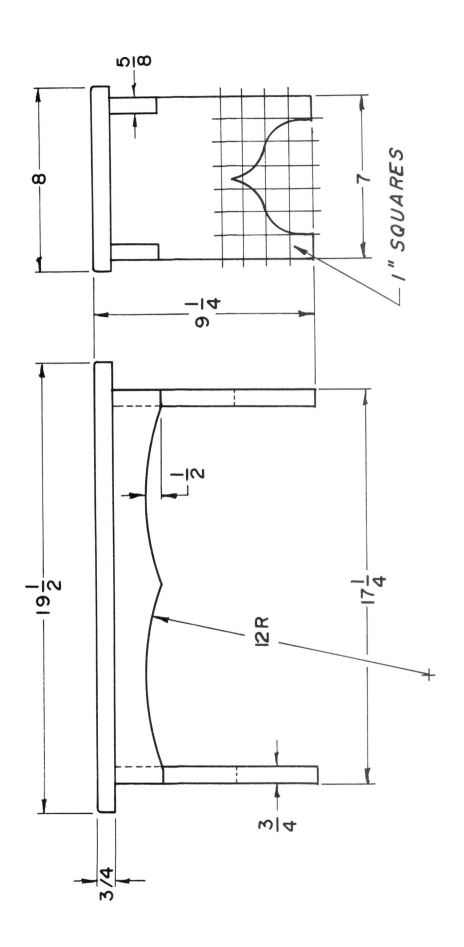

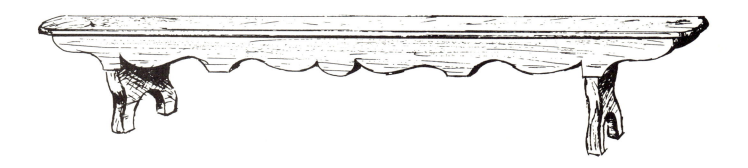

LONG STOOL—VERMONT
Pine—top and legs (outside only)
Natural—top and side supports—old red paint

BENCH—NEW HAMPSHIRE
Maple—natural finish

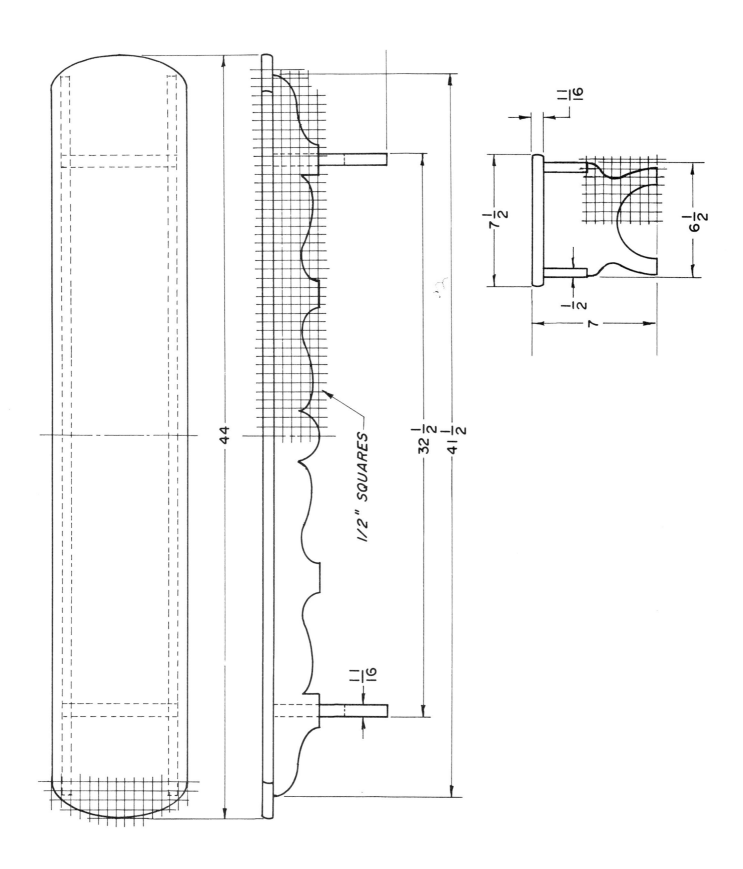

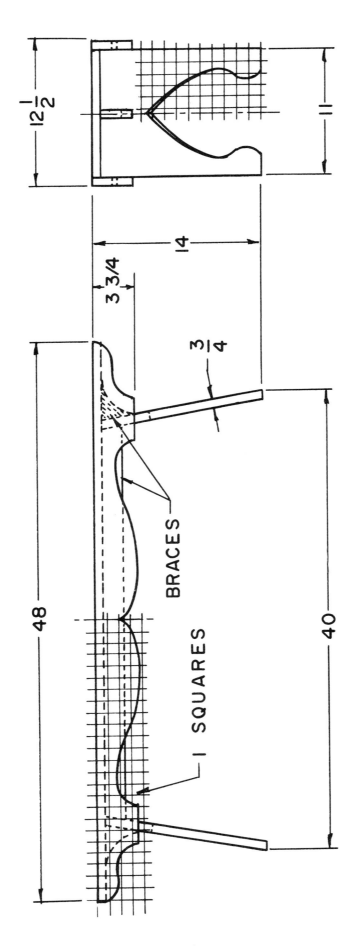

Slant-Lid Podium

This 1890 podium has a slant lid that lifts up. original had a brightly painted grain finish.

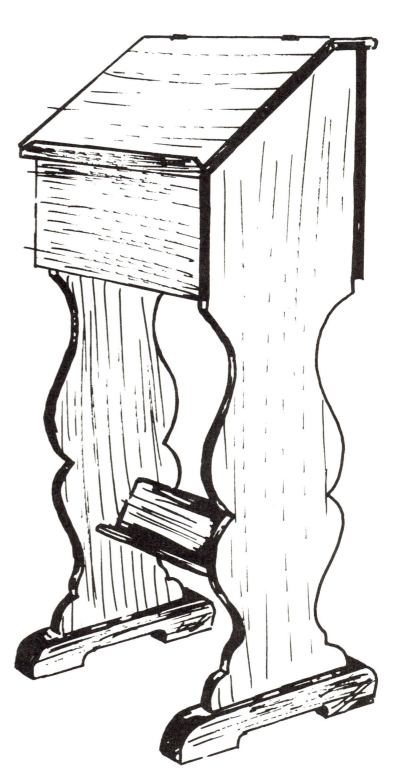

PODIUM WITH SLANT LID
Spruce—painted grain finish

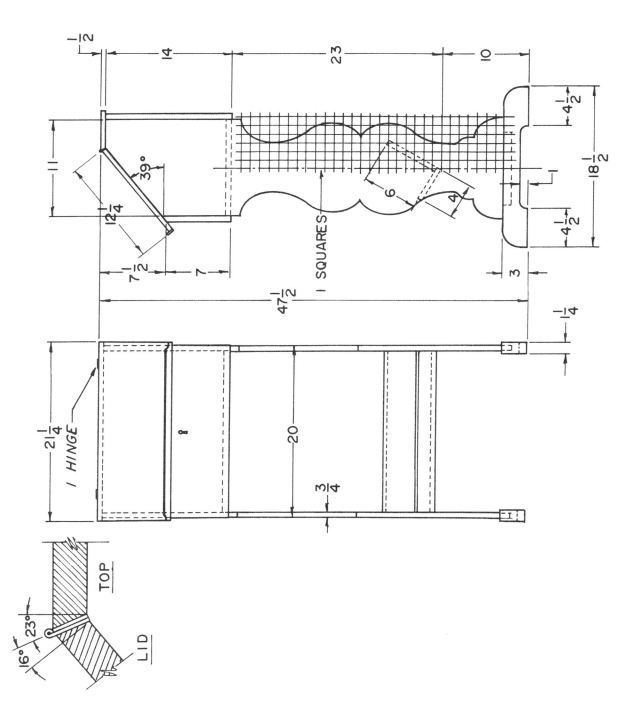

Saw Horse

This unusual saw horse provided a storage area for various woodworking tools. Today it could be used as a shelf for plants.

SAW HORSE WITH STORAGE AREA
Maple—natural finish

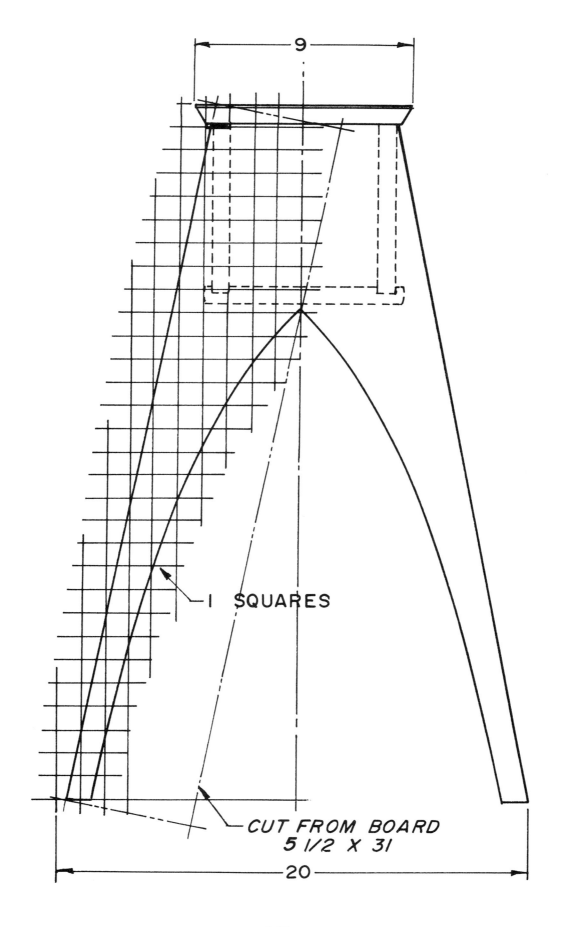

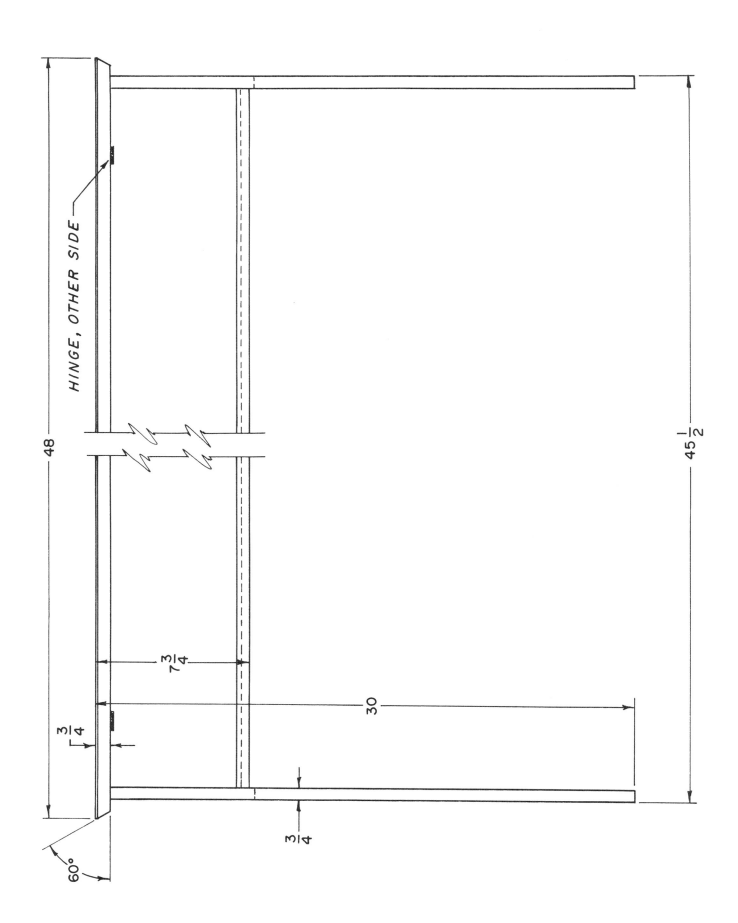

150

Bucket Bench

An outstanding Pennsylvania bucket bench is illustrated. This one has scalloped and semicurved sides. The original was painted a mustard yellow.

BUCKET BENCH—PENNSYLVANIA
Pine—mustard paint

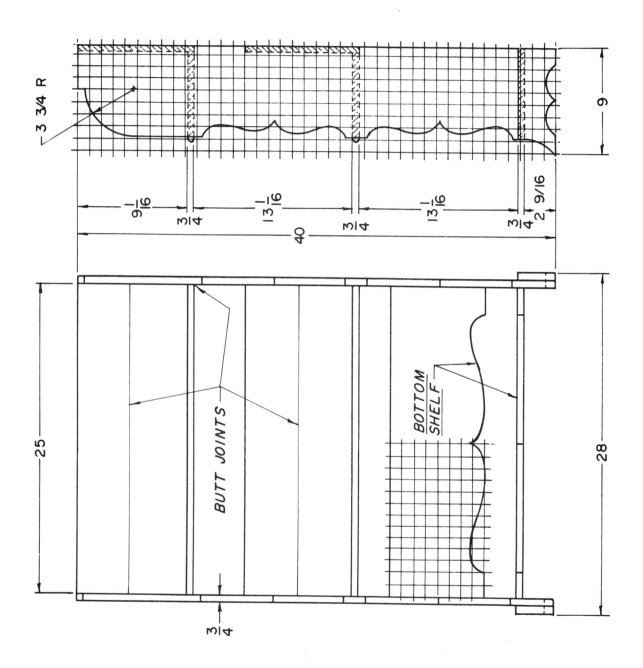

Dry Sink

Dry sinks were made to serve a need at a given point in time. Each is unique. Some were simple and had only shelves; others had doors. Most were made of pine.

DRY SINK WITH STEPBACK DRY SINK—c 1820
Pine—old red paint

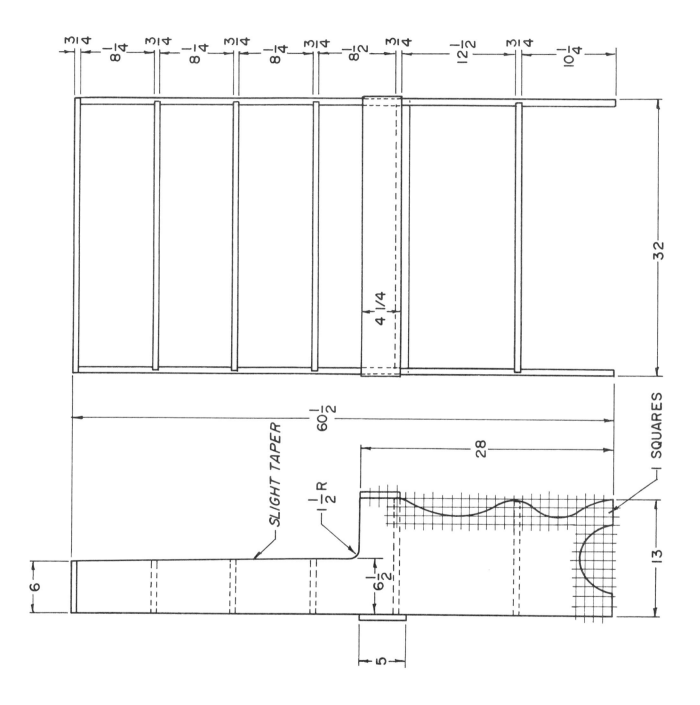

DRY SINK WITH RAISED-PANEL DOORS
Pine—light blue paint

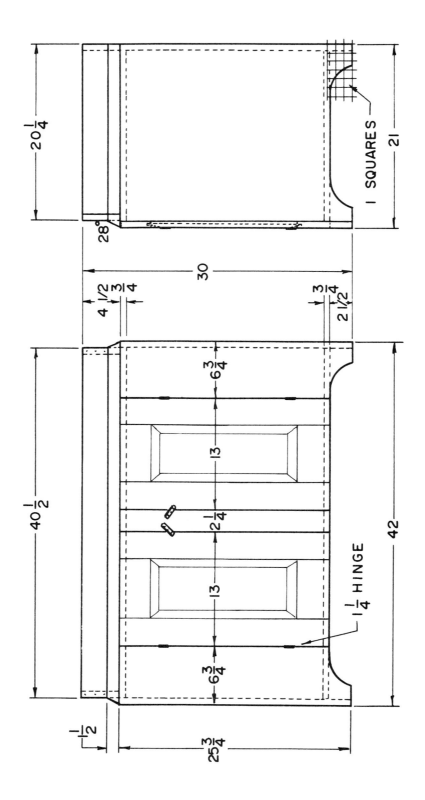

DRY SINK
Pine—natural finish

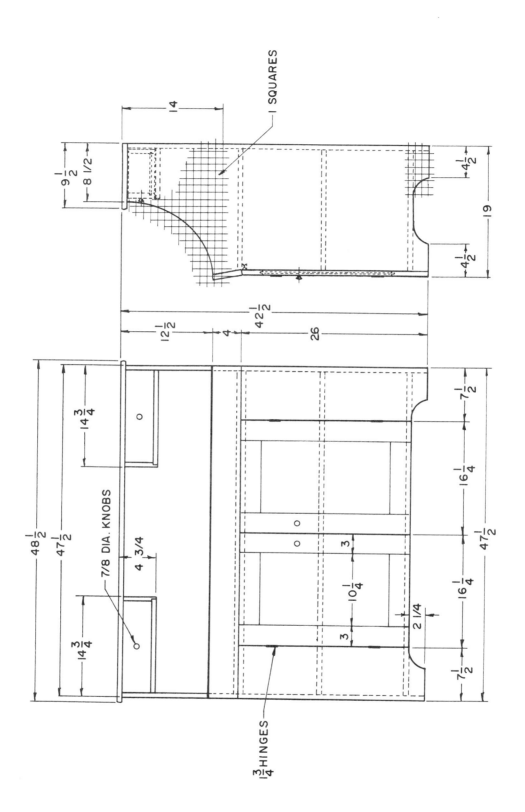

Dough Box

Dough boxes, as the name implies, were used to mix and knead bread. Many dough boxes did not have legs and were brought to the ingredients for mixing. It is not uncommon to find legs attached to a portable dough box so it could be used as a table.

DOUGH BOX WITH LEGS
Pine—with a dark stain

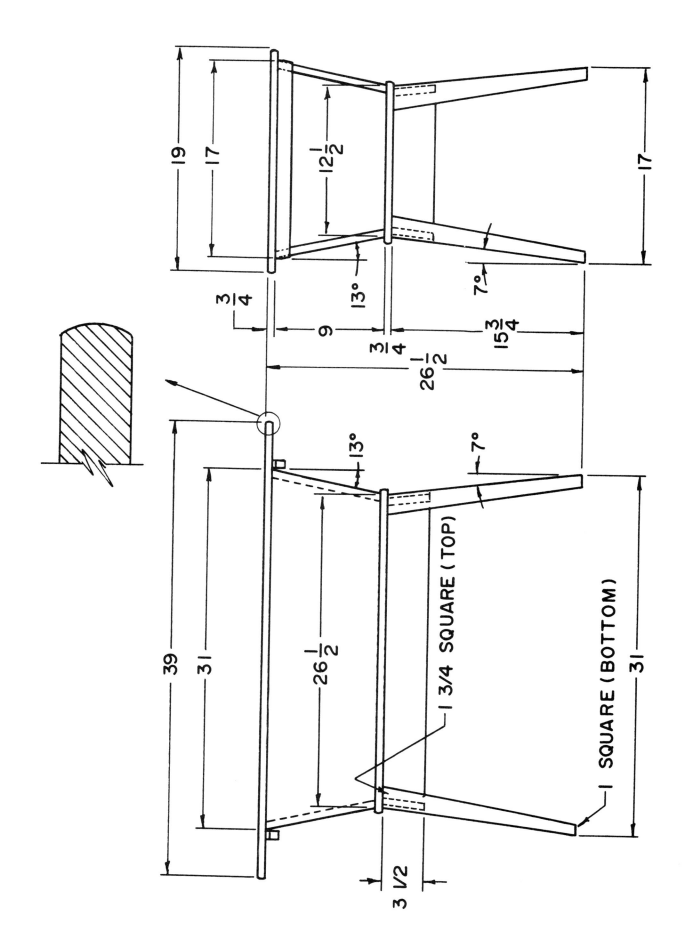

Miniature Cupboard

This example is a small storage cupboard with bootjack ends, a handy place to store all those odds and ends you don't know just what to do with.

**MINIATURE CUPBOARD
WITH BOOTJACK ENDS**
Pine—gray paint

CUPBOARD WITH RAISED PANEL DOORS
Walnut—natural finish

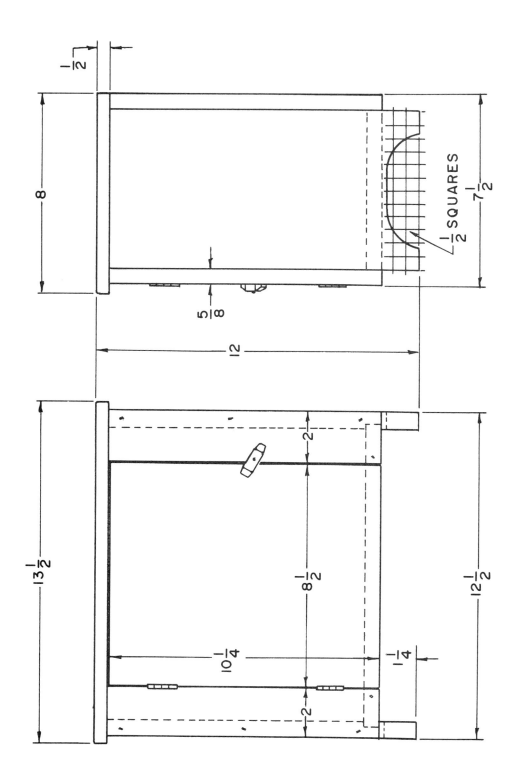

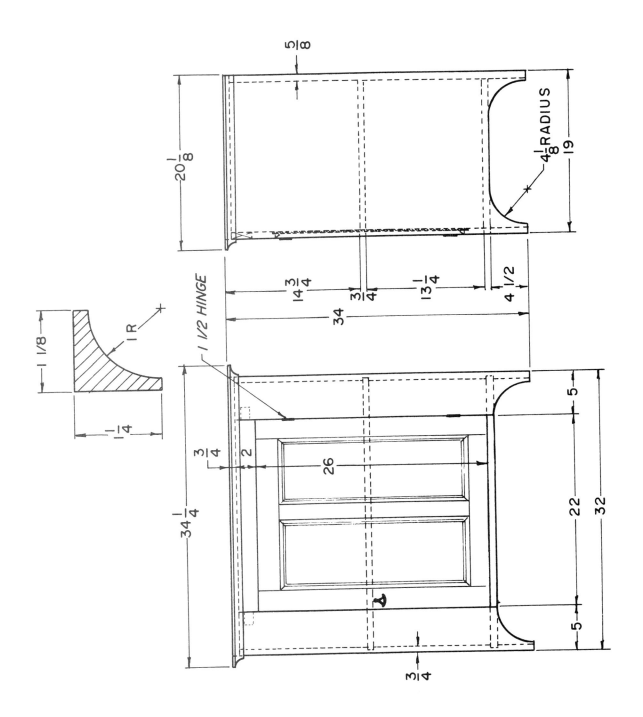

Grain Bin

The grain bin of yesterday makes an excellent wood box for today. This example is from Pennsylvania and is tongue and groove construction.

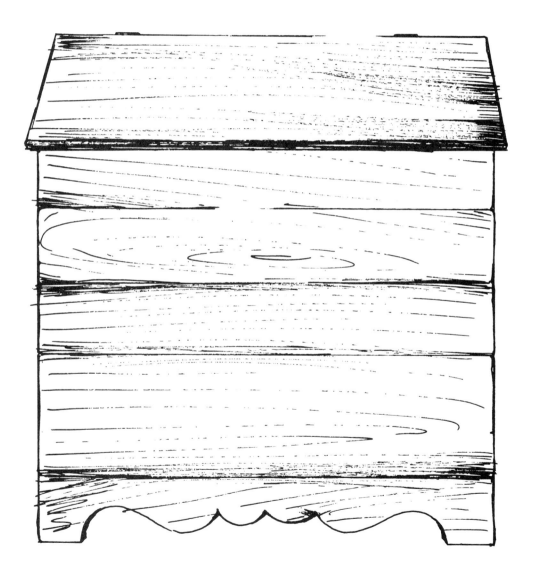

GRAIN BIN—PENNSYLVANIA
Spruce—light gray paint

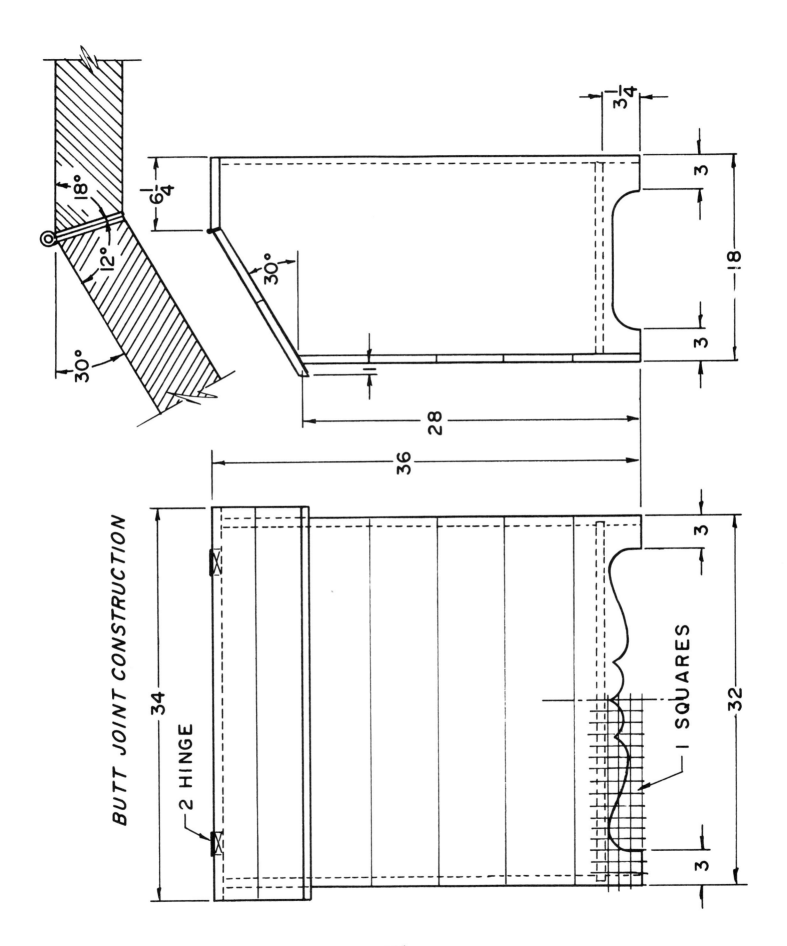

Tables

Early American tables were large and heavy. Many were made of thick oak and were over 6 feet long, with thick, turned legs. Other woods such as maple, cherry, walnut, and poplar were used also. As time passed, many other table designs were used. In the end, the Pilgrim, harvest, and sawbuck styles prevailed and are still popular today.

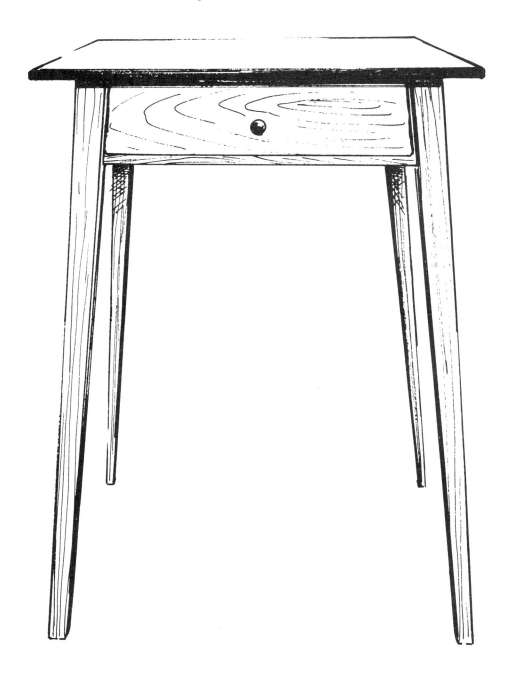

SPLAY LEG TABLE WITH SINGLE LONG DRAWER
Maple—natural finish

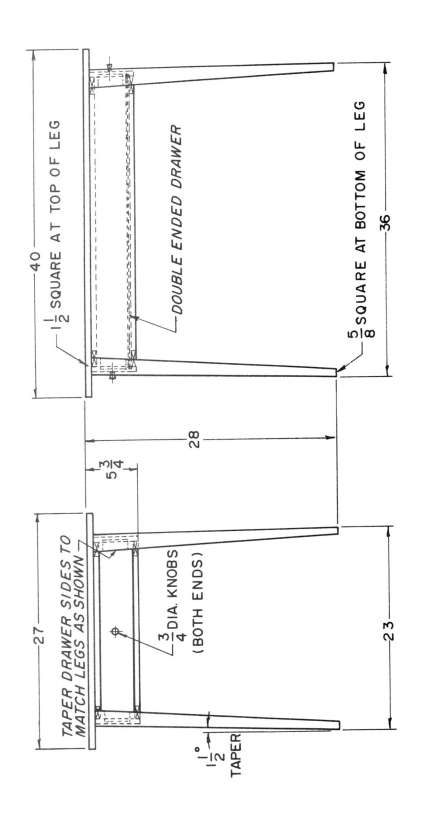

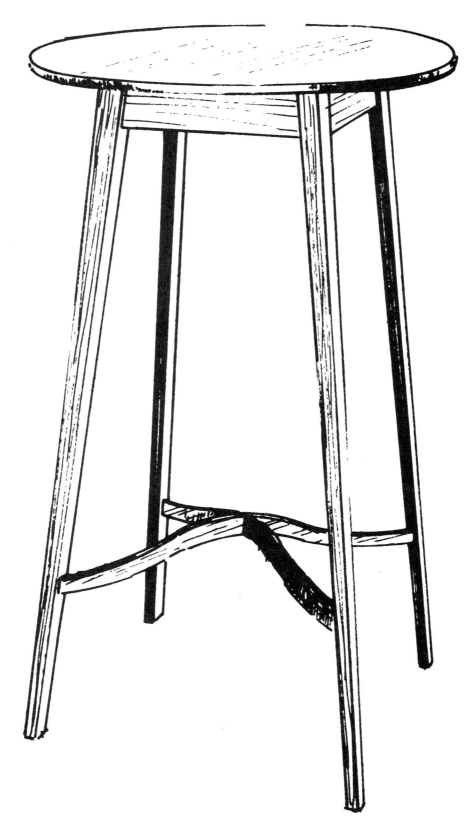

TEA TABLE—SHERATON STYLE—c 1790
Mahogany—natural finish

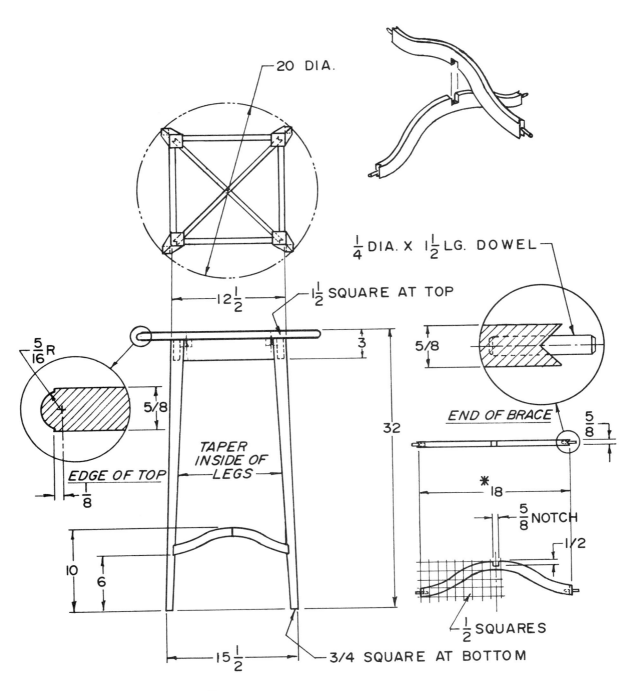

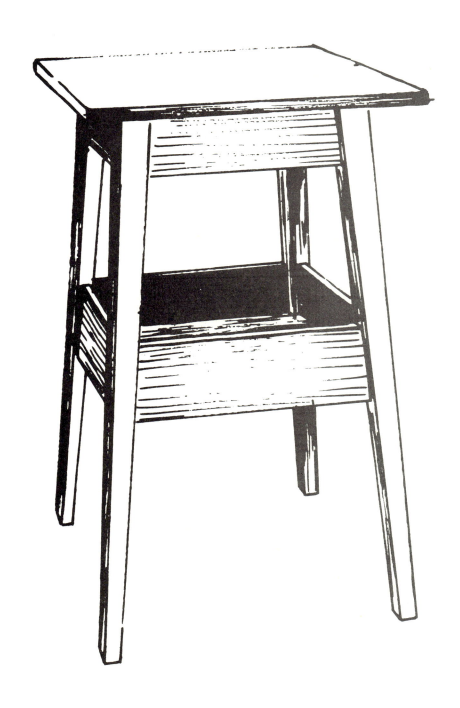

SPLAY LEG STAND—MASSACHUSETTS—c 1800
Pine—with painted grain

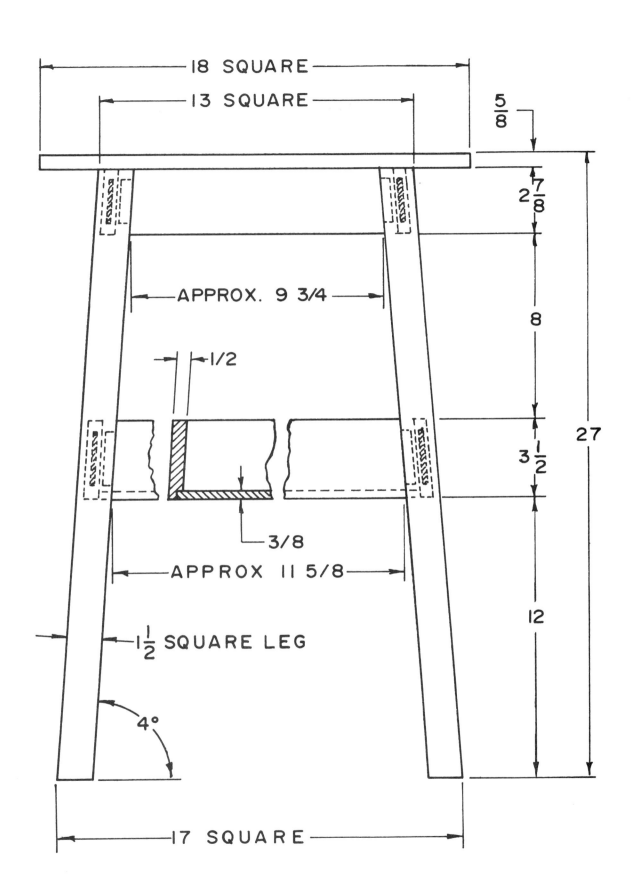

SPLAY—LEG CANDLE STAND WITH APRON—c 1875
Pine—natural finish

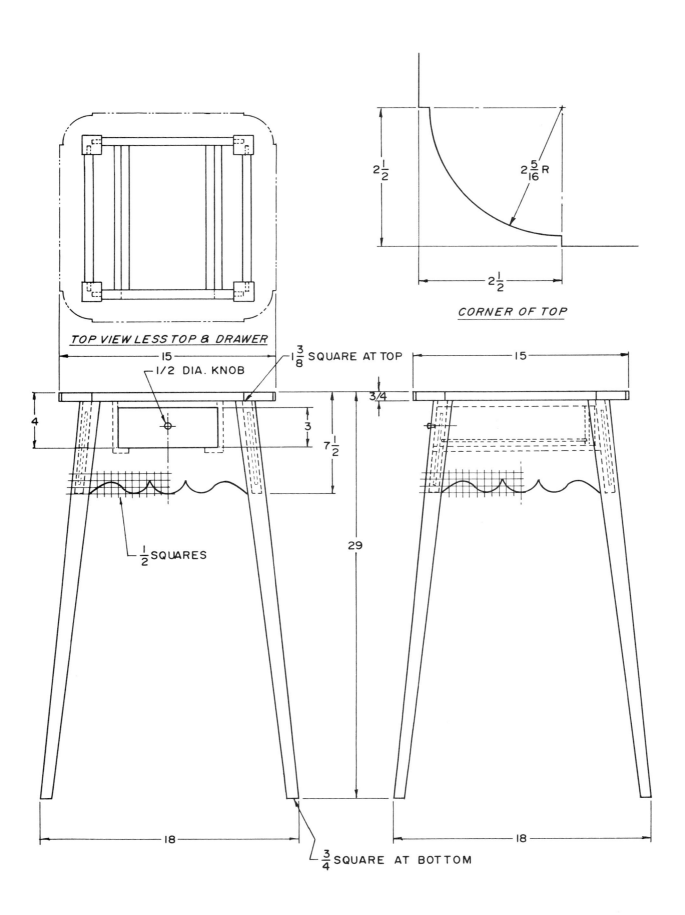

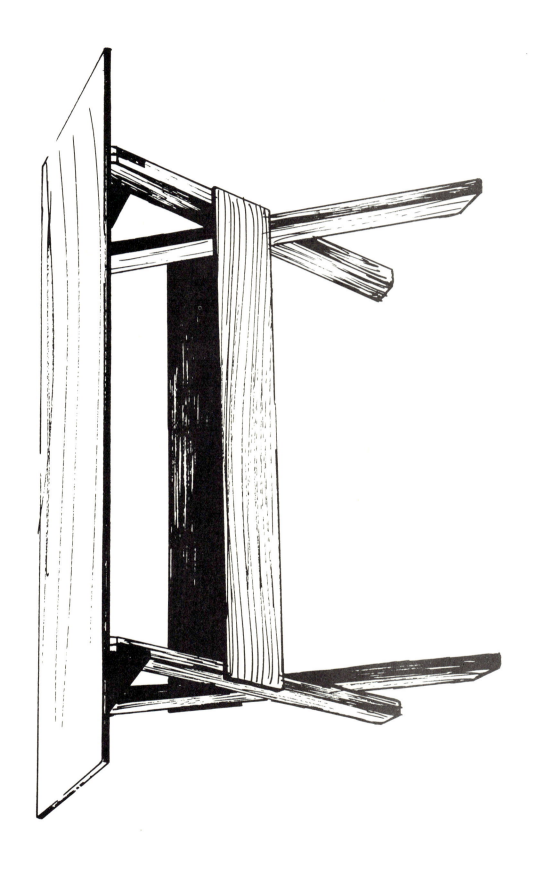

SAWBUCK TABLE—c 1795
Pine—old red paint

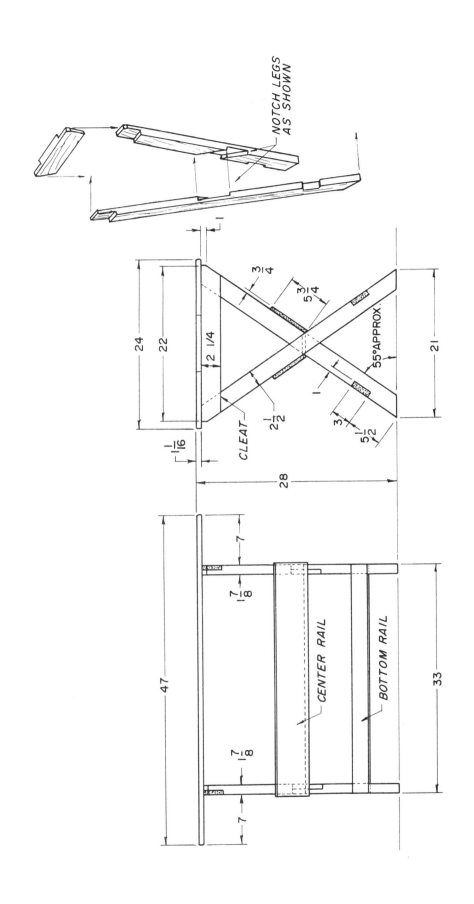

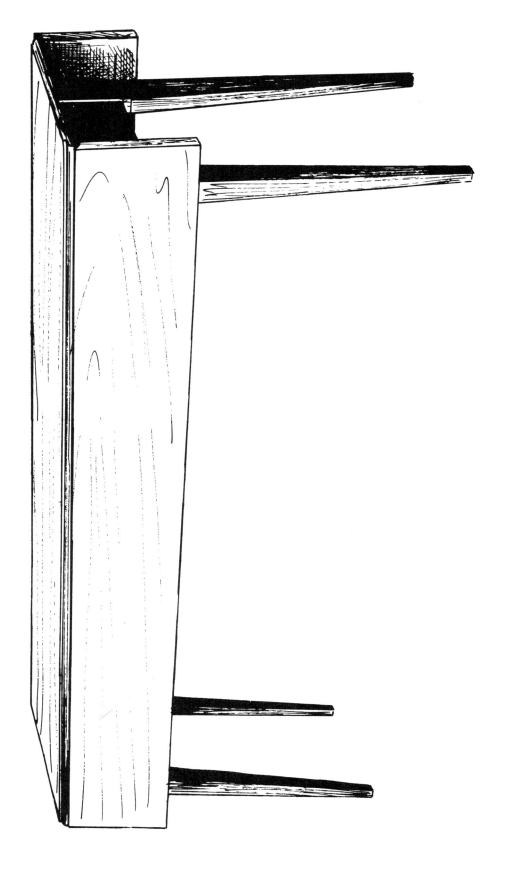

HARVEST TABLE—c 1785
Maple—natural finish

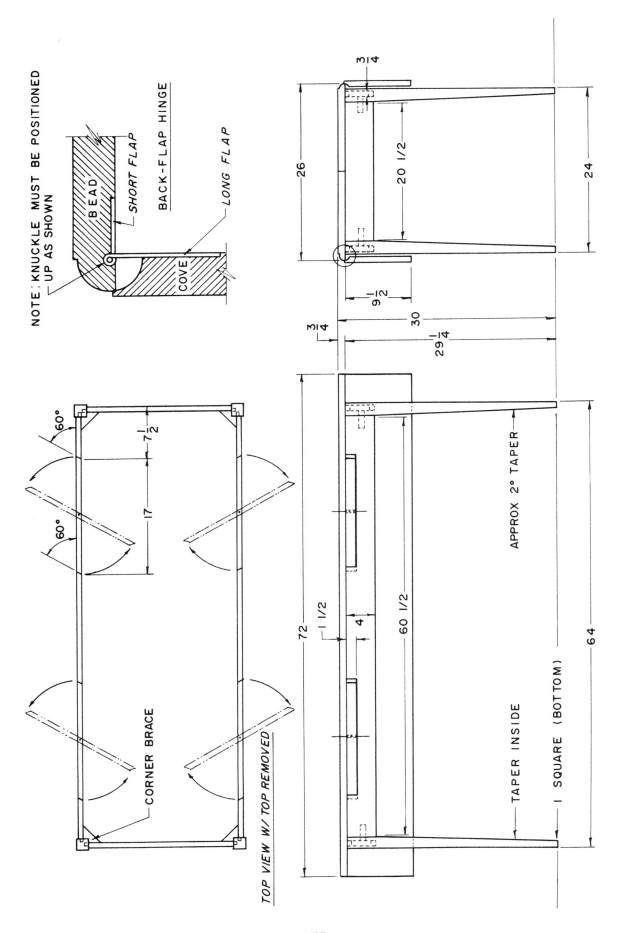

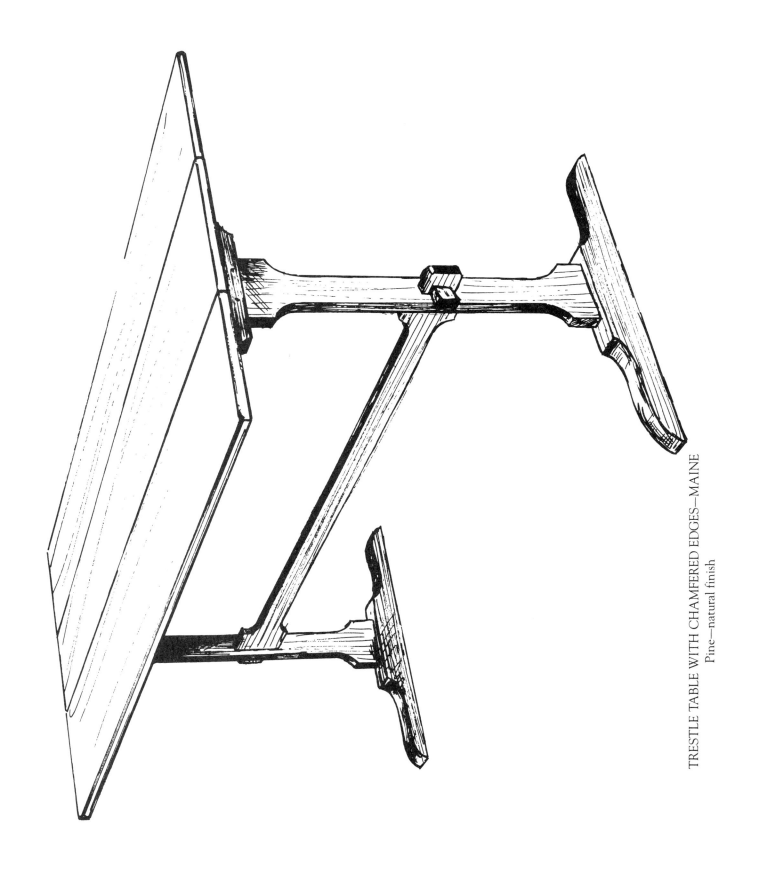

TRESTLE TABLE WITH CHAMFERED EDGES—MAINE
Pine—natural finish

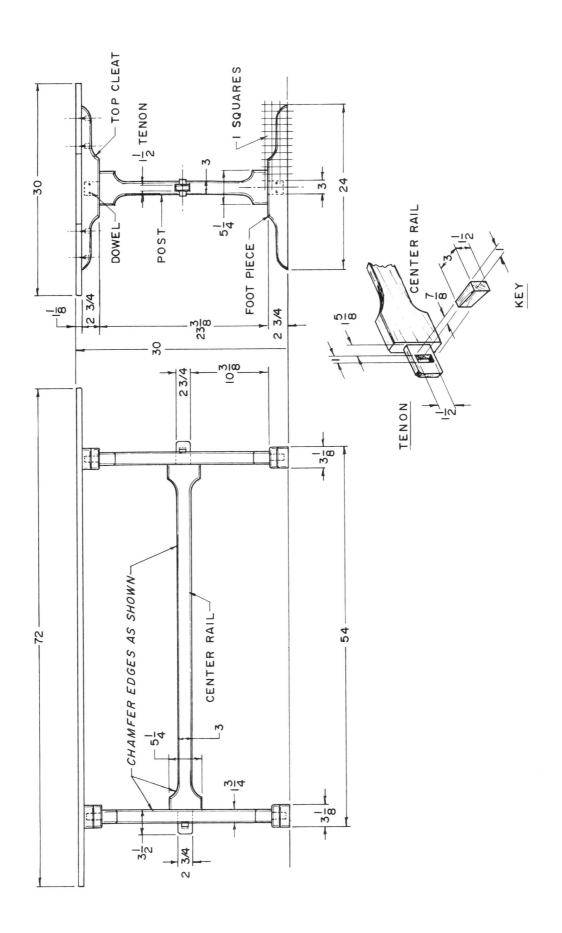

Chairs

There were many kinds of chairs made: ladder-back, pressed-back, kitchen, wicker, and rocking chairs are just a few. The earliest American chairs were made of oak with large, bulbous sausage turnings. By 1700 pine and hardwood ladder-back chairs were being made. The ladder-back chair is so called because of the several curved horizontal back boards.

Early chairs were made with dried horizontal members and green, unseasoned wood for all vertical members. The green vertical members had holes or slots drilled into them to accept the dry horizontal members. As the unseasoned wood dried, it shrank and locked itself around the horizontal pieces, forming a tight, unglued joint.

CAT CHAIR
Maple—painted black and red

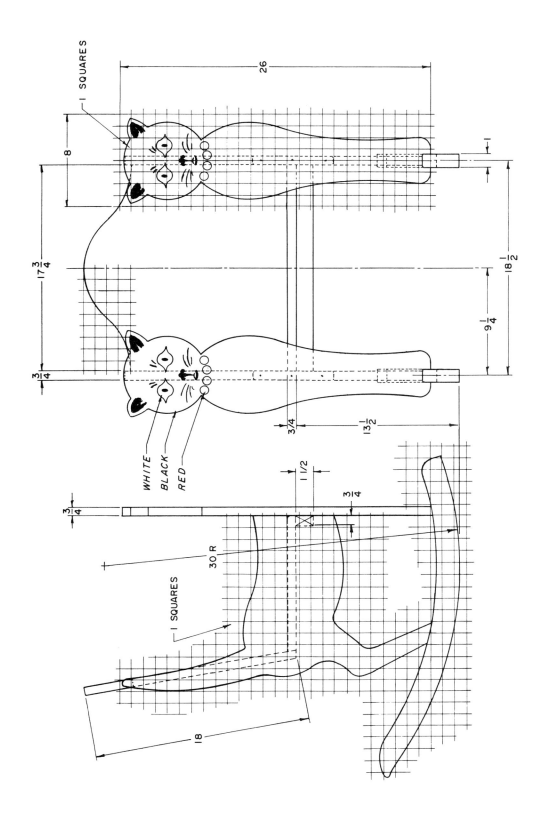

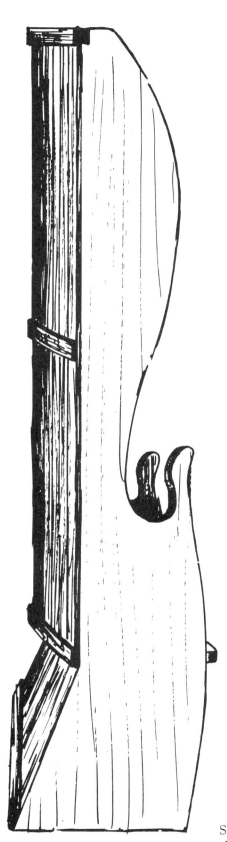

SETTEE—VERMONT
Pine—very dark stain

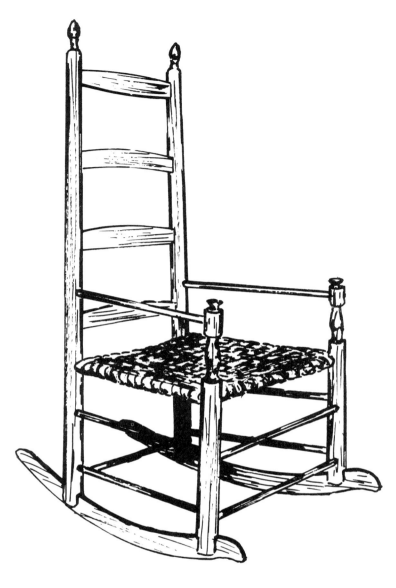

ROCKER—MAINE
Maple—old red paint

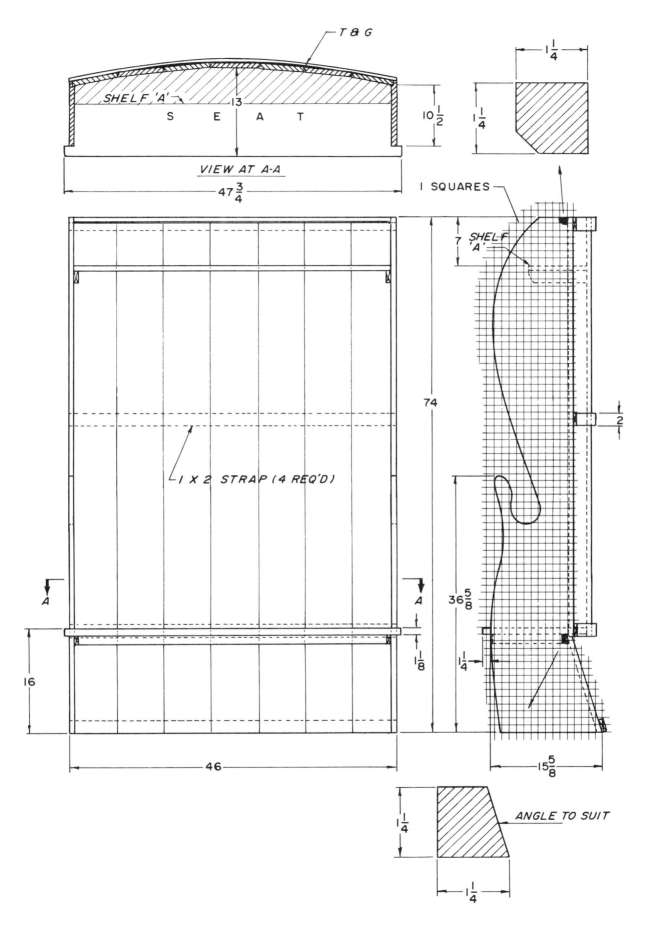

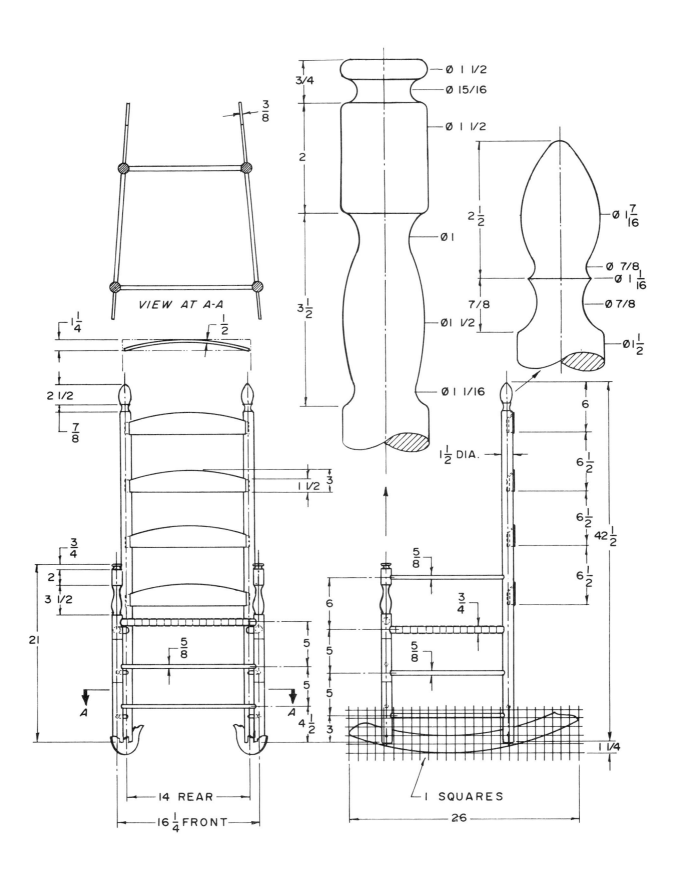

Chests

The chest is perhaps the earliest piece of what we now call furniture. Case furniture suggests a case or box style of construction. From the simple six-board chest came the one-drawer chest, the three-drawer chest, the full chest of drawers, and finally cabinets, cupboards, desks, and the like. Compare the simple six-board chest with the full chest of drawers and you will see the similarity.

The first piece of furniture the Pilgrims made was the chest. These chests were used for storage, a bench to sit on, a table, or for travel. The earliest chests were simply made of six wide, pine boards. They were actually no more than wood boxes with hinged lids. They were, and still are, referred to as a six-board chest. The various chests in this text give examples of the many kinds of chests used in years past. Chests came in all sizes, from a very small desk box to rather large ones. Legs were later added to the simple box chest, then drawers, and eventually the simple box chest was a full chest of drawers. The ultimate in chests of drawers was the highboy.

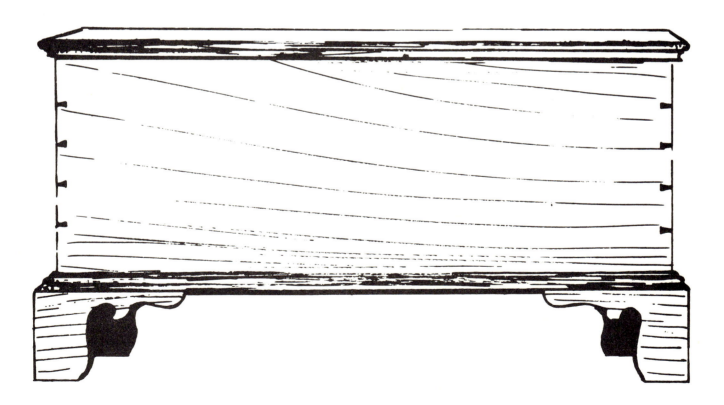

SMALL BLANKET CHEST WITH BRACKET FEET—c 1810
Pine—light blue paint

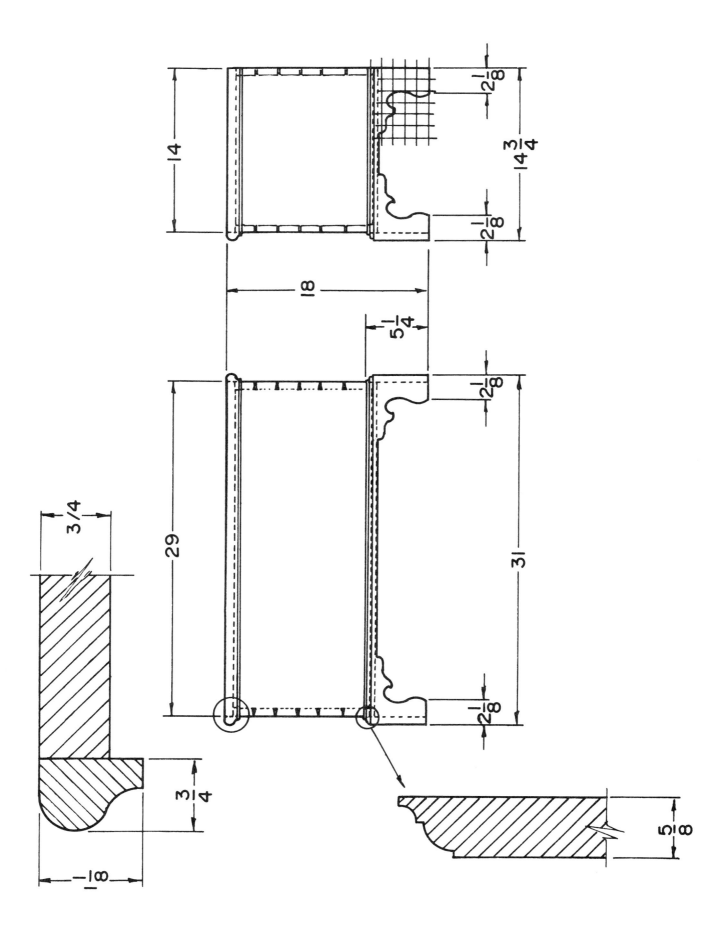

CHIPPENDALE BLANKET CHEST—NEW ENGLAND—c 1805
Dovetail joints
Pine—light blue paint

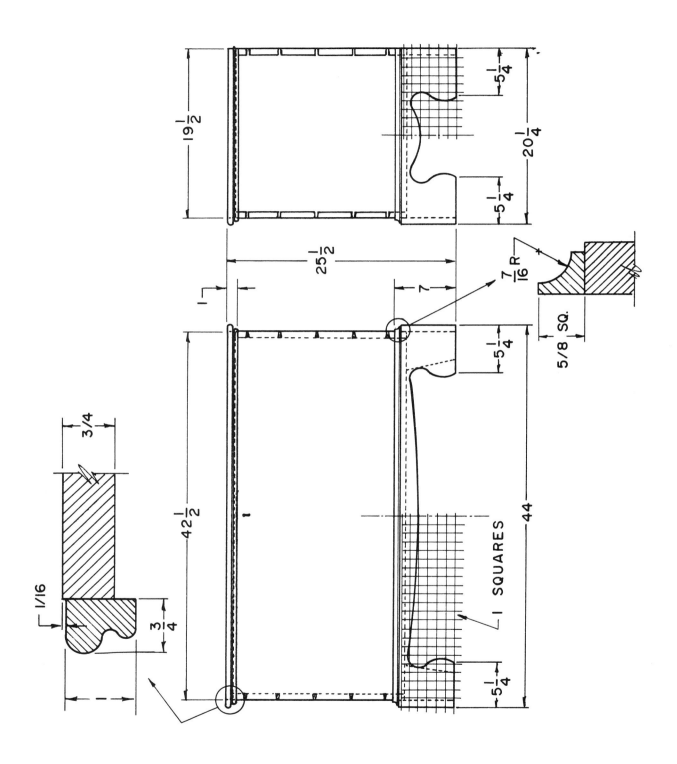

QUEEN ANNE ONE-DRAWER BLANKET CHEST—NEW ENGLAND—c 1755
Snipe hinges, square cut nails, wooden knobs
Pine—old red paint

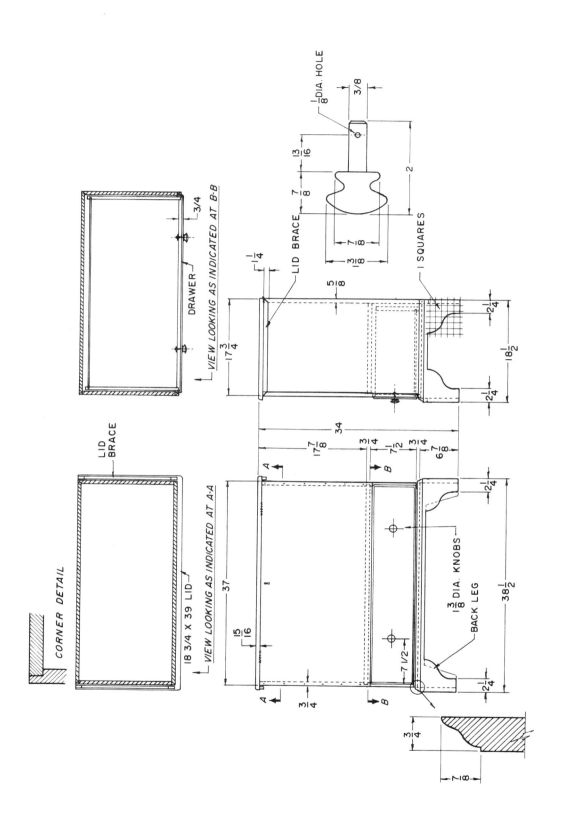

CHIPPENDALE THREE-DRAWER BLANKET CHEST—NEW HAMPSHIRE—c 1800
Snipe hinges, square-cut nails
Pine—blue paint

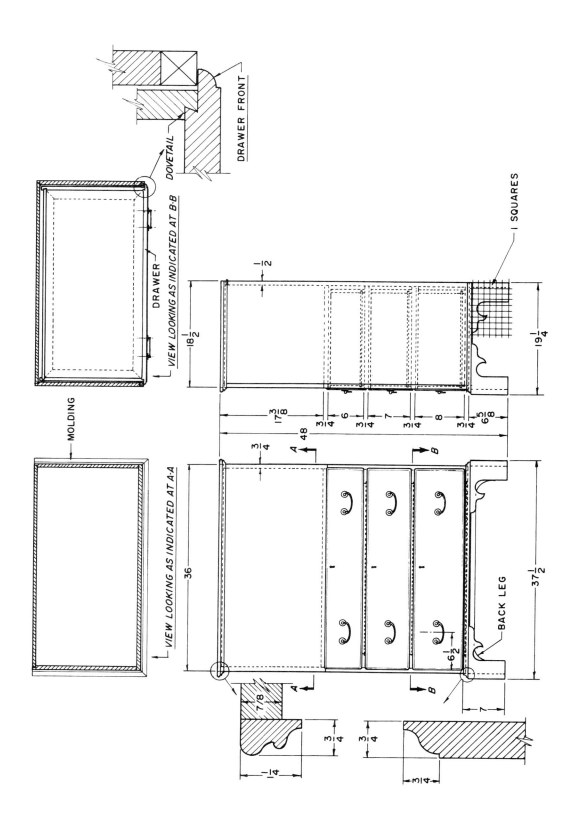

FULL CHEST OF DRAWERS—c 1850
Maple—dark stain

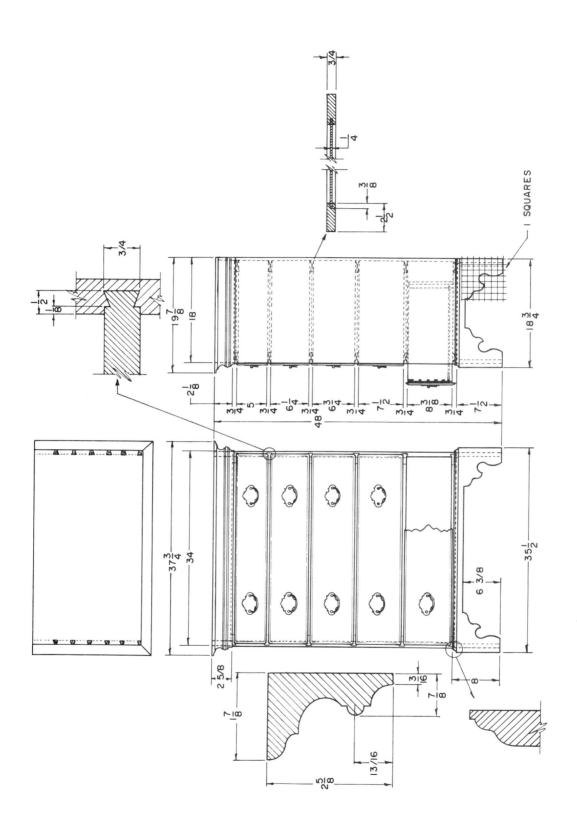

APOTHECARY CHEST OF DRAWERS
Pine—natural finish

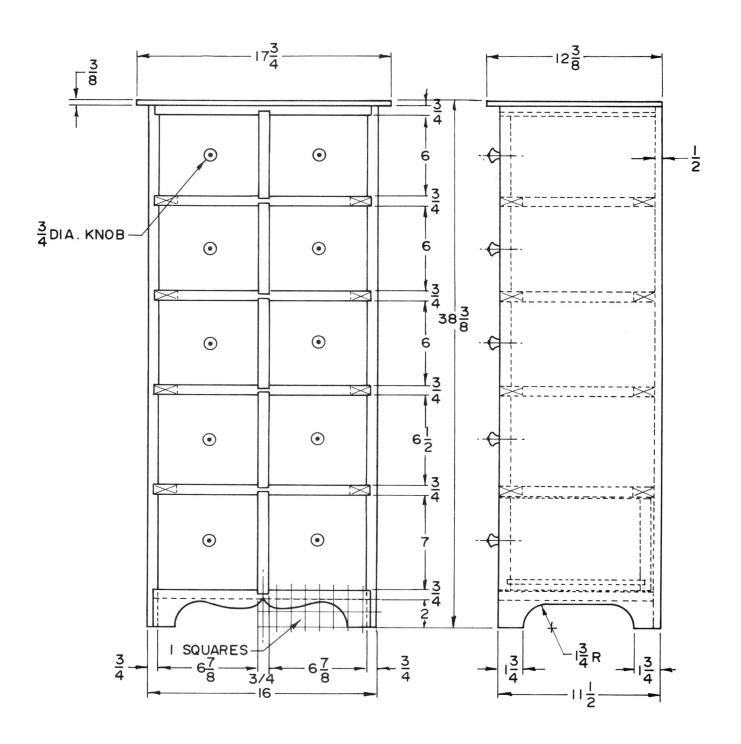

Lift-top Commode

Lift-top commodes can be found in most all antique shops. They must have been very popular and many must have been made. Oddly enough, all are about the same size and proportion. This was a take-off of a simple country chest. Today they are used throughout the house to store blankets, linens, clothes, and even toys. Some were constructed with dovetail joints; this particular one had only butt joints.

LIFT-TOP COMMODE WITH WOODEN KNOBS
Pine—natural finish

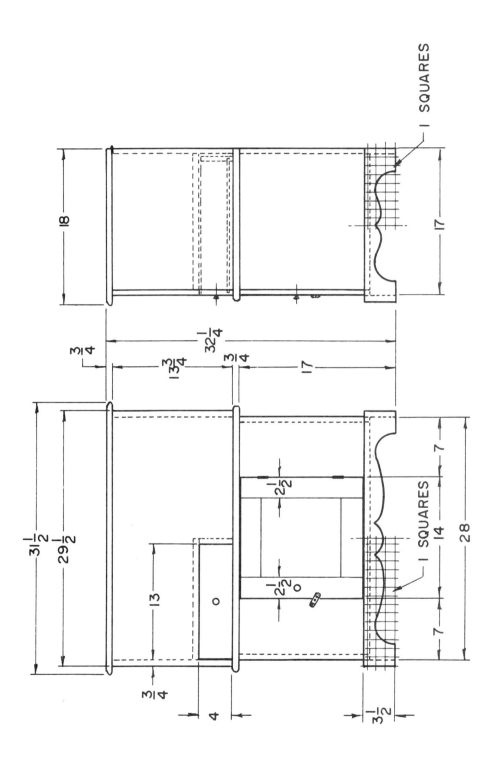

Wash Stand

This stand is Victorian and very gaudy. The sides were sponge-painted mustard yellow and brown. The rest was mustard yellow with thin black and red line striping. The floral pattern on the backboard and drawer was set on a off-white background. If you have an antique pitcher and bowl set, this may be just the right piece to display your set—but it is unusual!

VICTORIAN WASH STAND
Pine and maple—painted surfaces

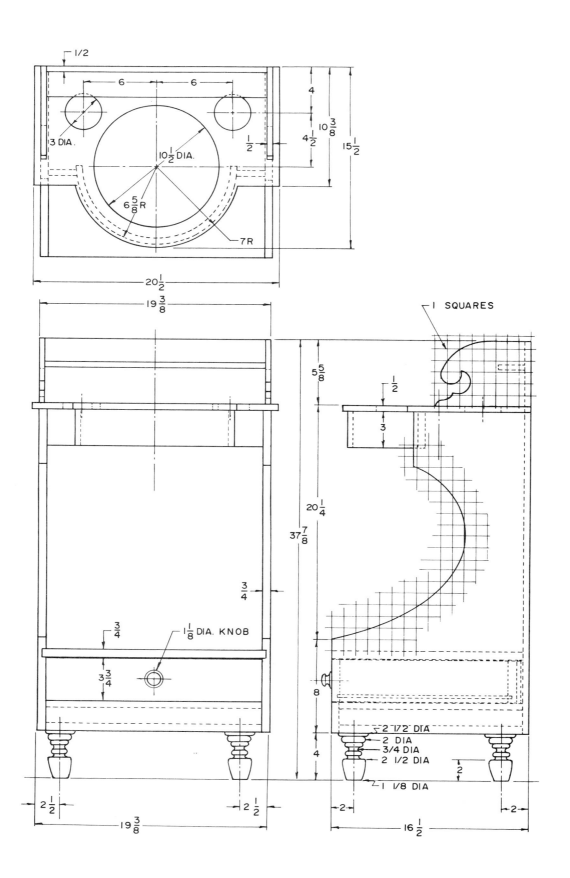

Formal Pieces

Straying slightly from the "country" and "primitive" pieces are these two formal projects. Perhaps they do not belong in a book with the other pieces, but they were so beautiful and unusual. I couldn't resist.

One is a formal cabinet with a drawer, made of butternut. The other is a lowboy chest of drawers on legs made of cherry in Connecticut.

DOCUMENT CABINET WITH DRAWER
Butternut—natural finish

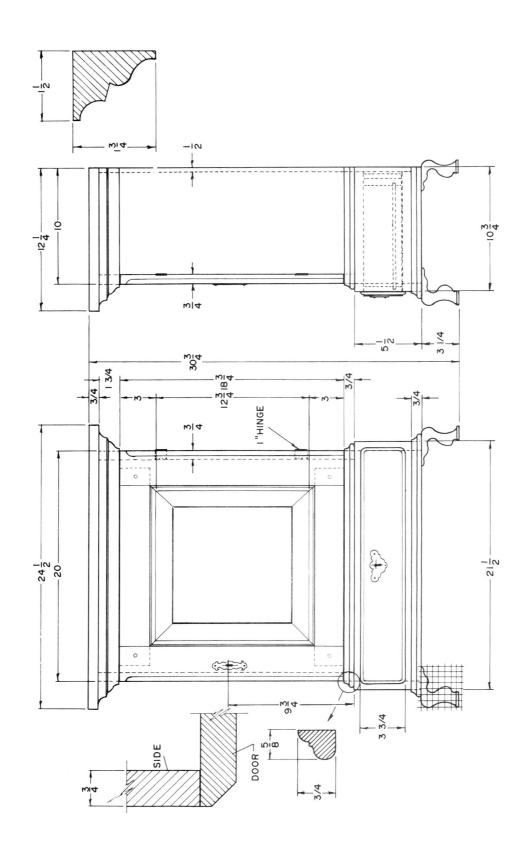

LOWBOY—NEWPORT STYLE
Cherry—natural finish

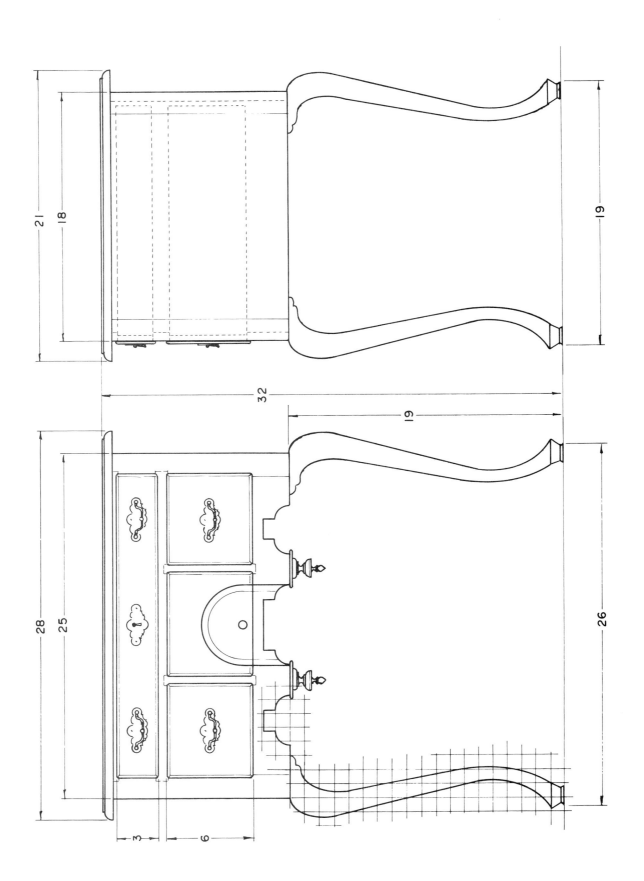

Pewter Hutches

As pewter and pottery plates began to replace wooden plates, the pewter hutch became very popular. At first rails were used to hold the plates vertically; later grooves replaced the rails. These cupboards had two or three open shelves at the top to display the pewter and a closed cupboard underneath with one or two shelves. As years passed, pewter cupboards gave way to the more formal china cabinets of the 1800s, as low-priced pressed glass replaced pewter and pottery.

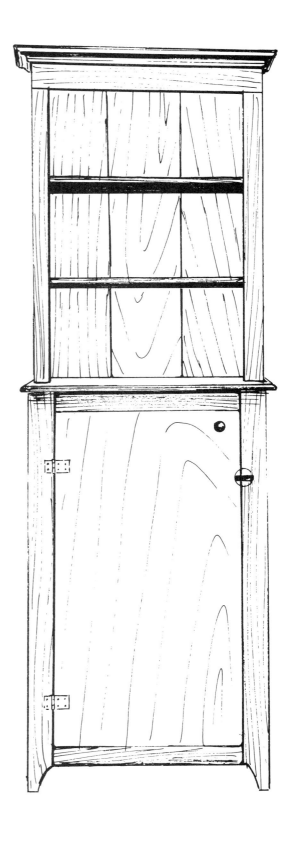

NEW ENGLAND STEPBACK CUPBOARD
WITH SMALL WOODEN DOORKNOB—c 1810
Pine—with brownish paint

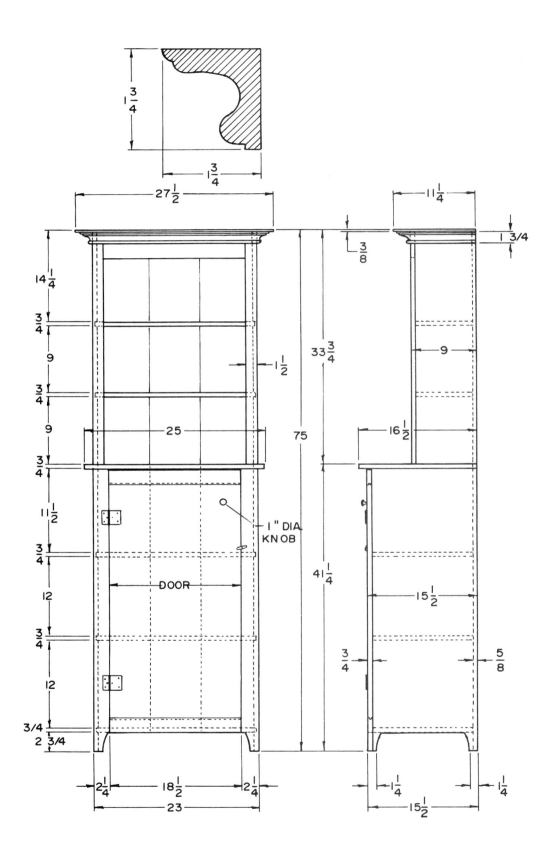

COUNTRY HUTCH—c 1840
Pine—old red paint

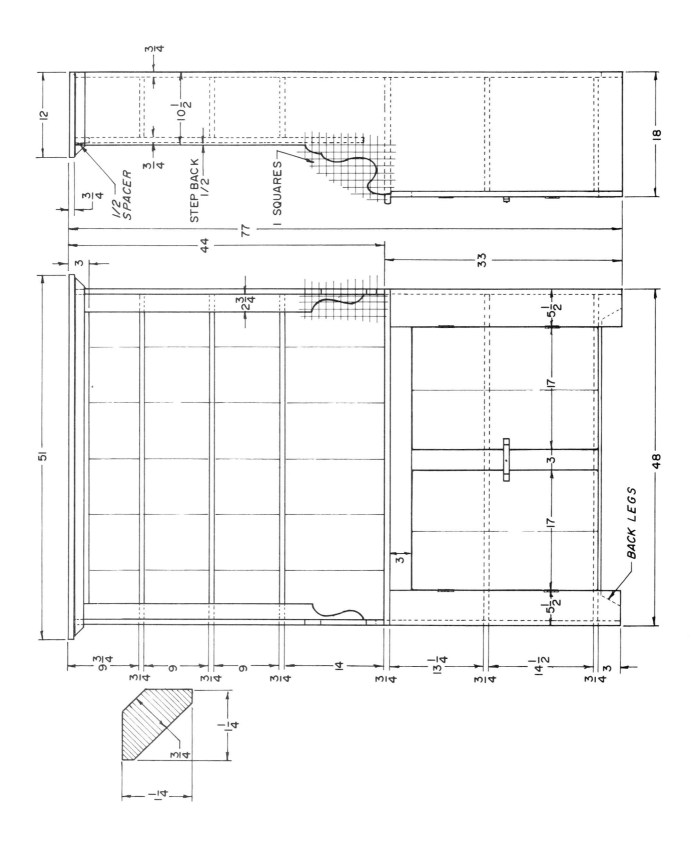

COUNTRY STEPBACK CUPBOARD—c 1835
Pine—natural finish

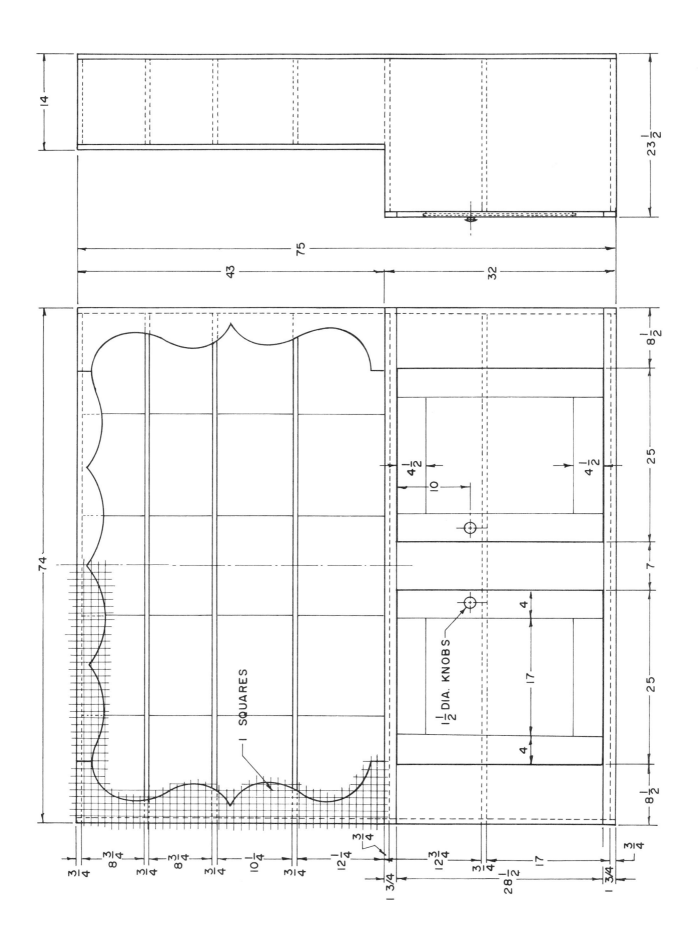

Beds

No book would be complete without at least one bed. Most home shops cannot make Colonial beds because of the high posts usually associated with early beds. This particular bed was chosen over the many beautiful Early American beds because of its simplicity. Most home lathes have a 36-inch capacity and should be able to turn the four posts—the longest being only 32¼ inches high. The actual size should be altered slightly to accommodate today's springs and mattresses. The original was made of hardwood and painted red. There is beauty in its simple design.

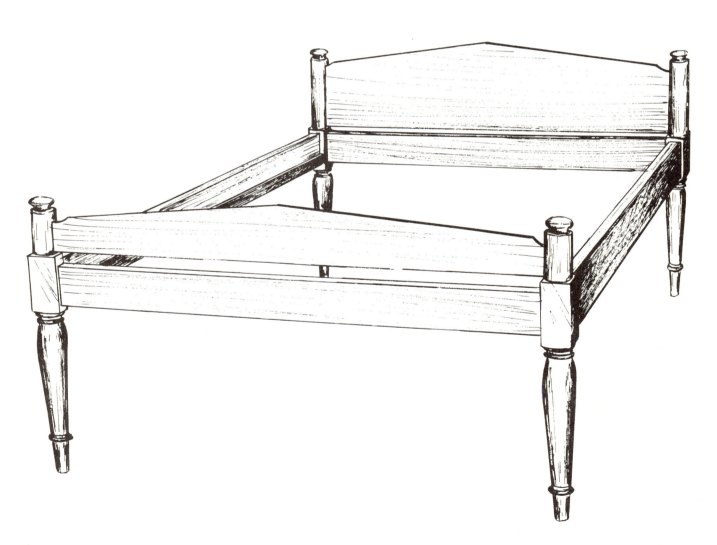

LOW POST BED (ORIGINAL ROPE BED)—c 1810
Maple—old red paint

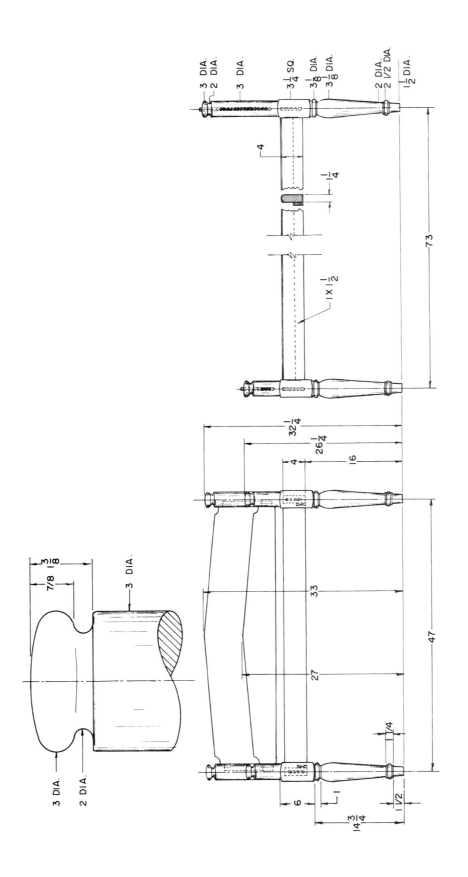

Cupboards

Like built-in wall shelves of today, closets were not usually included in the houses of yesterday. The cupboards served this function. Most of these were also one of a kind and built for a particular room or area. They came in all shapes and sizes. The most interesting, I think, is the bonnet chest, sometimes called a chimney cupboard. It was very thin and very tall. It is very unusual but extremely functional today, as it does not take up much floor space, but it does have a *lot* of shelf space.

CUPBOARD
Pine—yellow paint

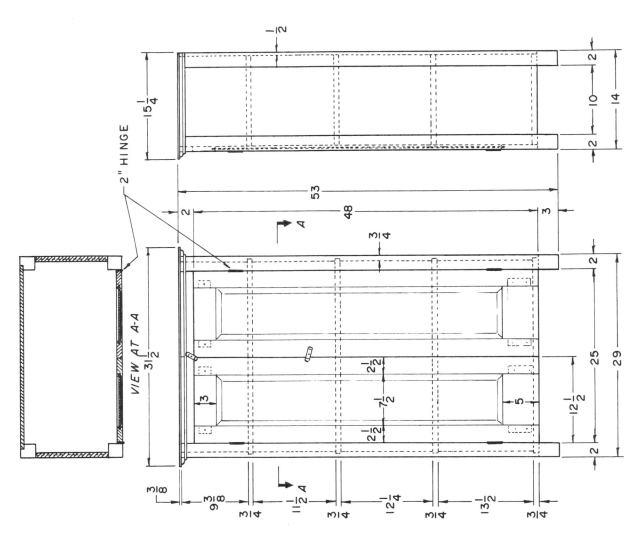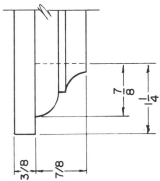

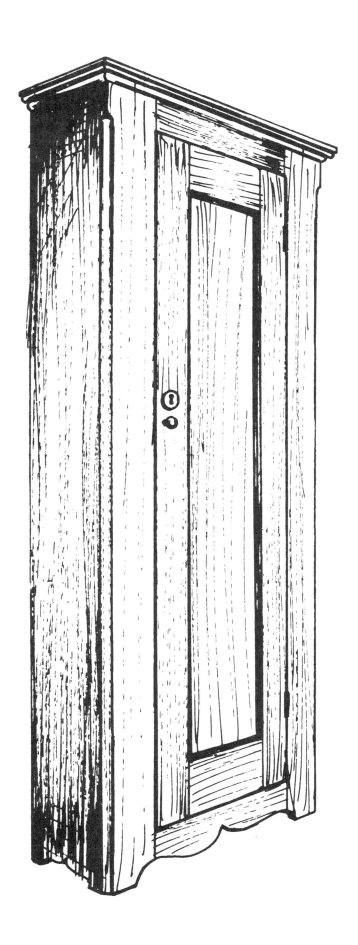

CHIMNEY CUPBOARD—RHODE ISLAND—c 1810
Pine—red paint (some graining effect)

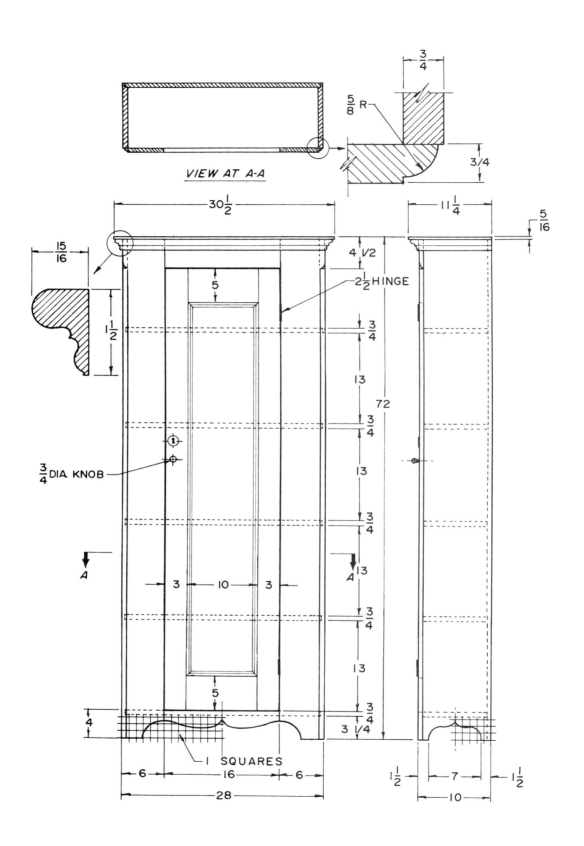

BONNET CHEST WITH WOODEN KNOB
Maple—natural finish

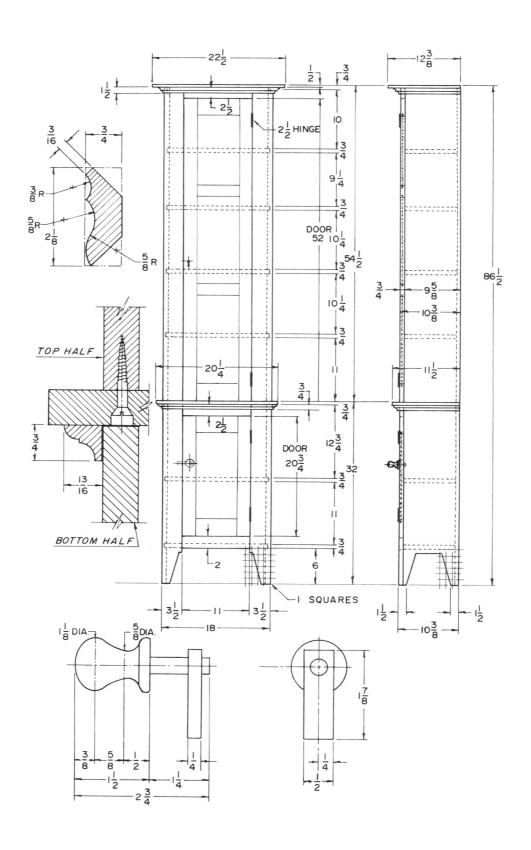

Tall Case Clocks

Almost everyone is attracted to the tall case clock known as a grandfather clock and would like to own one. It adds beauty, warmth, charm, and substance to any home. Through the years it has been a hallmark stating that its owner has achieved a certain level of success. A tall case clock is a very special woodworking project and will last much longer than you will and probably will be passed on to your children and grandchildren. It is truly a prized possession.

Today, the price of an antique clock such as this is extremely prohibitive. The original of this particular model, made by Eli Terry in 1802, at Plymouth, Connecticut, would probably cost well over $8,000, *if* it could be purchased. It had a one-day wooden movement with a printed paper dial. A good reproduction costs well over $1,500 and probably would have a plywood or pressed-wood back. The original was made of pine, therefore the case will cost from $35 to $55 today, depending on the kind of hardware used. A quality grandfather clock movement costs from $175 to $450, therefore your clock would cost from $200 to $500. Recommended movement: La Rose Inc. #084069, with a 42 inch pendulum drop and a cast bell similar to that of yesterday. This is a very low cost in today's "plastic" world, plus you will take much pride in building a project such as this. This is one woodworking project that will add life to any home. It will soon become part of the family.

The dial can be purchased from any one of the suppliers listed under "Clock Supplies" in the Appendix, but it is not difficult to make your own out of ¼-inch-thick wood. Paint the wood an off-white and add a light wash coat around the edges for that "aged" look. Lay out the face with a drafters' technical pen. (See figure 86-8.) The movement is supported on a shelf between the two side boards of the case. Two short boards, ⅝ x 1½ x 6 inches secured to the case will hold the shelf. If the recommended movement is used, the shelf, as illustrated in figure 86-9, will support the movement and allow for the weights to hang through the slot. The two ¼-inch holes will secure the movement to the shelf. The shelf is then simply set on the two boards attached to the side boards. Attach the pendulum and weights. Adjust the "crotch" (the arm at the rear of the movement that is attached to the pendulum rod) so the pendulum will "tick" and "tock" at an equal distance from the center of the

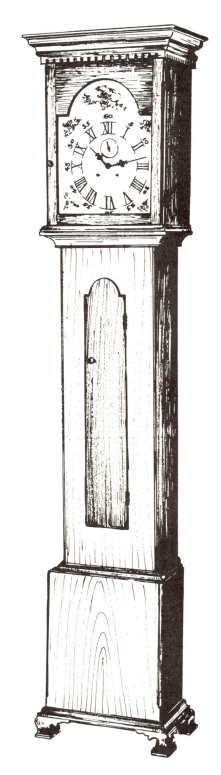

TALL CASE CLOCK BY ELI TERRY—c 1802
Pine—dark stain finish

clock. This is a called "putting the clock into beat"—it should "tick" and "tock" evenly. The clock speed is adjusted by raising or lowering the pendulum (*up* to speed the clock up, *down* to slow it down). Test the clock for 24 hours or so—if it's all right, attach the face, hands, and hood to the clock. The clock should give you years of satisfaction and add a lot of warmth to your home.

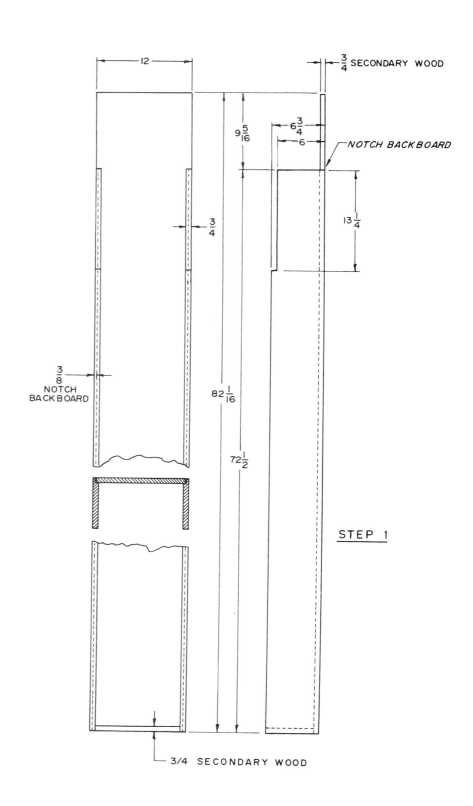

STEP 1—CASE

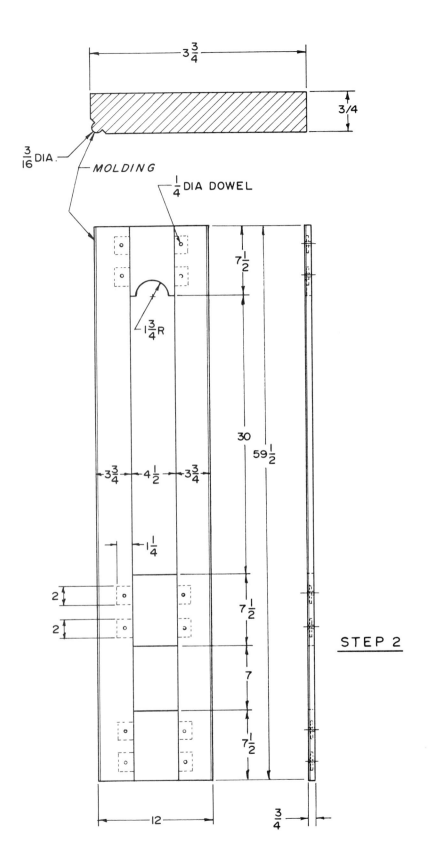

STEP 2—FRONT PANEL

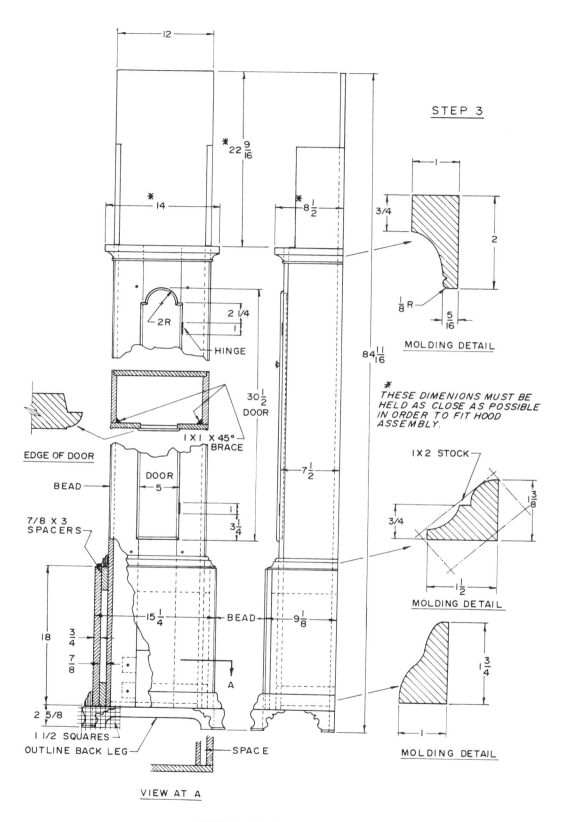

STEP 3—CASE ASSEMBLY

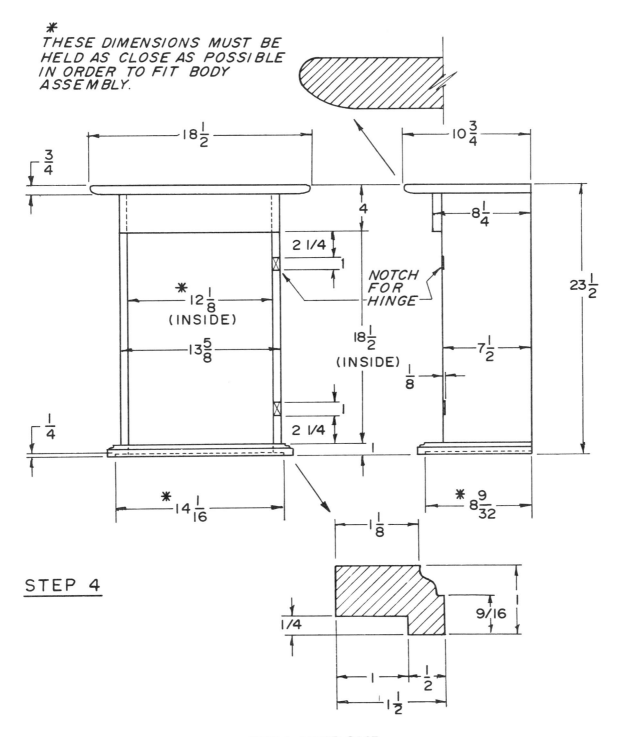

STEP 4—HOOD CASE

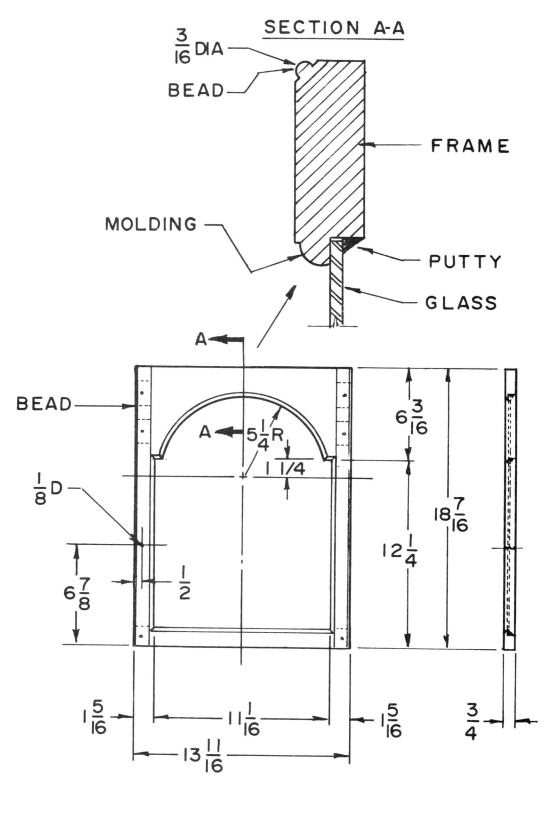

STEP 5—HOOD DOOR ASSEMBLY

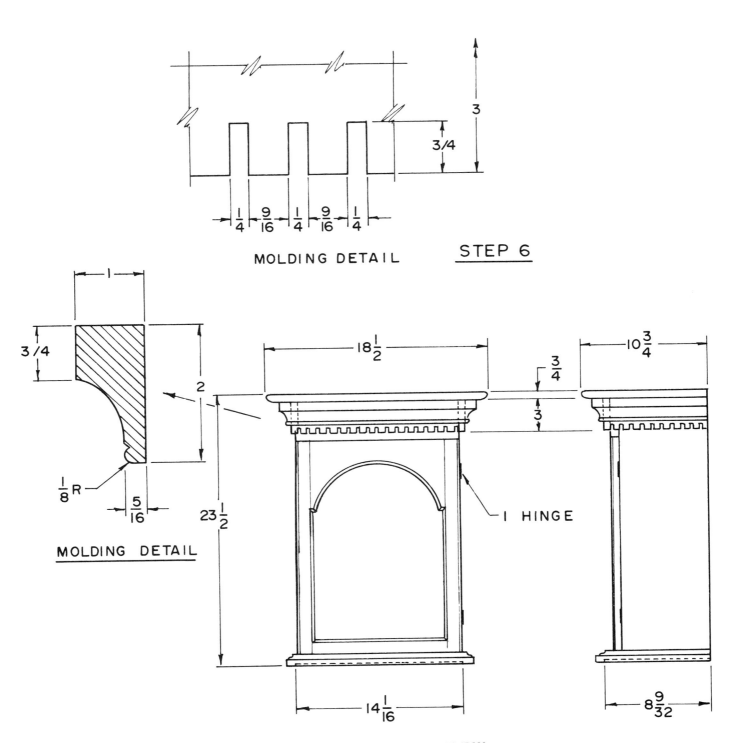

STEP 6—COMPLETE HOOD ASSEMBLY

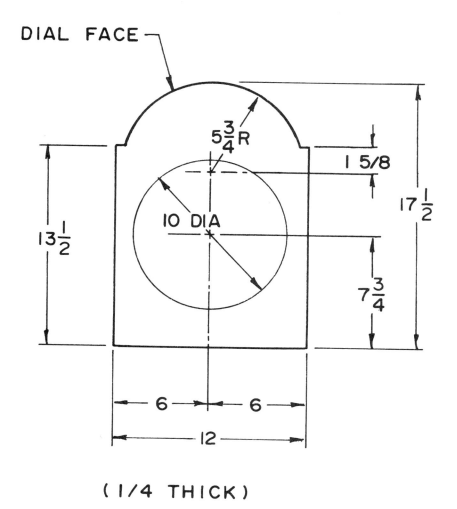

STEP 7

DIAL BLANK

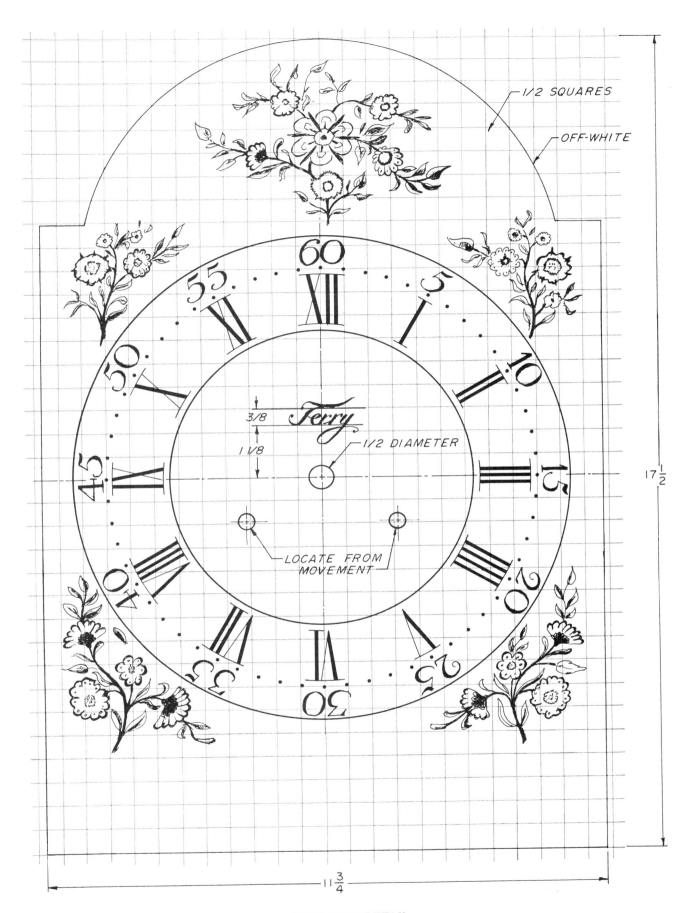

DIAL FACE DETAIL

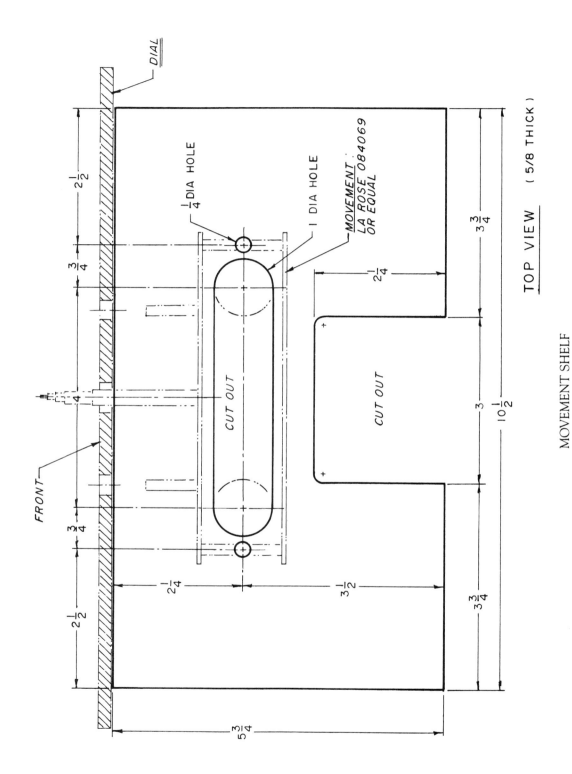

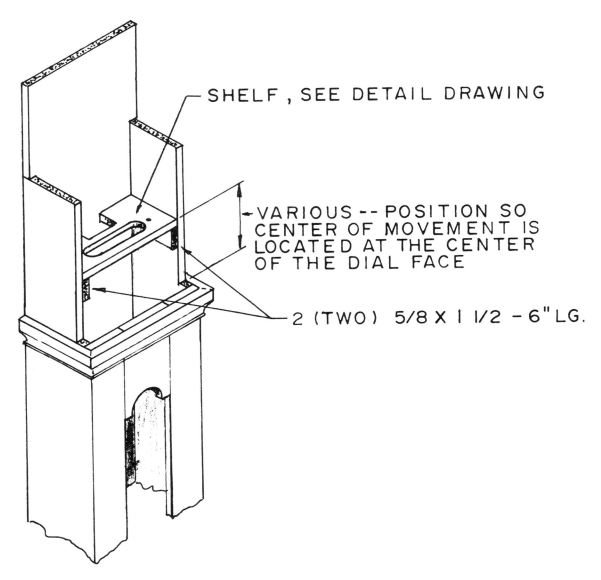

ADDING SHELF TO CASE

Part V

Appendix

Antique Hardware and Accessories Suppliers

PAINT

Cohassett Colonials
Cohasset, MA 02025

Stulb Paint and Chemical Co. Inc.
P. O. Box 297
Norristown, PA 19404

MILK PAINT

The Old-Fashioned Milk Paint Co.
Main St.
Groton, MA 01450

Stulb Paint and Chemical Co., Inc.
P. O. Box 297
Norristown, PA 19404

STAINS/TUNG OIL

Cohassett Colonials
Cohasset, MA 02025

Deft Inc.
17451 Von Darman Ave.
Irvine, CA 92713-9507

Formby's Inc.
825 Crossover Lane
Suite 240
Memphis, TN 38117

Stulb Paint and Chemical Co., Inc.
P. O. Box 297
Norristown, PA 19404

Watco-Dennis Corp.
Michigan Ave. & 22nd St.
Santa Monica, CA 90404

OLD-FASHIONED NAILS/BRASS SCREWS

Equality Screw Company Inc.
P. O. Box 1296
El Cajon, CA 92022

Horton Brasses
P.O. Box 95
Nooks Hill Rd.
Cromwell, CT 06416

Tremont Nail Co.
21 Elm St.
P.O. Box 111
Wareham, MA 02571

BRASSES

Ball and Ball
463 West Lincoln Hwy.
Exton, PA 19341

The Brass Tree
308 N. Main St.
Charles, MO 63301

Garrett Wade Company Inc.
161 Avenue of the Americas
New York, NY 10013

Heirloom Antique Brass Co.
P.O. Box 146
Dundass, MN 55019

Horton Brasses
P.O. Box 95
Nooks Hill Rd.
Cromwell, CN 06416

Imported European Hardware
4295 S. Arville
Las Vegas, NV 89103

Mason and Sullivan Co.
586 Higgins Crowell Rd.
West Yarmouth
Cape Cod, MA 02678

19th Century Co. Hardware Supply Co.
P.O. Box 599
Rough and Ready, CA 95975

The Renovators' Supply
Millers Falls, MA 01349

Ritter and Son Hardware
Dept WJ
Gualala, CA 95445

VENEERING

Bob Morgan Woodworking Supplies
1123 Bardstown Rd.
Louisville, KY 40204

GENERAL CATALOGS

Brookstone Co.
Vose Farm Road
Peterborough, NH 03458

Constantine
2050 Eastchester Rd.
Bronx, NY 10461

The Fine Tool Shops
20 Backus Ave.
P.O. Box 1262
Danbury, CT 06810

Leichtung Inc.
4944 Commerce Parkway
Cleveland, OH 44128

Silvo Hardware Co.
2205 Richmond St.
Philadelphia, PA 19125

Trendlines
375 Beacham St.
Chelsea, MA 02150

Woodcraft
41 Atlantic Ave.
P.O. Box 4000
Woburn, MA 01888

The Woodworkers Store
21801 Industrial Blvd.
Rogers, MN 55374

CLOCK SUPPLIES

H. DeCounick & Son
P.O. Box 68
200 Market Plaza
Alamo, CA 94507

S. LaRose Inc.
234 Commerce Pl.
Greensboro, NC 27420

Mason and Sullivan Co.
586 Higgins Crowell Rd.
West Yarmouth
Cape Cod, MA 02678

Merritt's Antiques Inc.
Rd. 2
Douglassville, PA 19518

STENCILING SUPPLIES

Adelle Bishop Inc.
Dorset, VT 05251

Related Publications and Organizations

The American Woodworker
JM Publications Inc.
13 Walton Mall
Box 1408
Hendersonville, TN 37075

Early American Life
P.O. Box 8200
Harrisburg, PA 17105

Fine Woodworking
The Taunton Press
52 Church Hill Road
Box 355
Newton, CT 06470

International Woodworking Magazine
Plymouth, NH 03264

Popular Woodworker
EGW Publishing Co.
1300 Galaxy Way
Concord, CA 94520

Woodsmith
2200 Grand Ave.
Des Moines, IA 50312

The Woodworkers Journal
517 Litchfield Road
P.O. Box 1629
New Milford, CT 06776

Workbench Magazine
Box 5965
Kansas City, MO 64110

Museums Where Antique Furniture Can Be Found and Studied

Clock Museum
Bristol, CT 06010

Colonial Williamsburg
P.O. Box C
Williamsburg, VA 23187

Farmer's Museum
Cooperstown, NY 13326

Henry Ford Museum and Greenfield Village
P.O. Box 1970
Dearborn, MI 48121

Maritime Museum
San Francisco, CA 94100

Old Sturbridge Village
Sturbridge, MA 01566-0200

Shelburne Museum
Route 7
Shelburne, VT 05401

Some other fine building and craft books from Stackpole Books

Prospecting for Old Furniture
Your guide to buying and restoring affordable antiques for your home. The author's tips on buying and refinishing popular antiques are illustrated by more than 100 detailed line drawings.
by Don Marotta

Masterpiece Furniture Making
Thirty projects described step-by-step, each designed and constructed with today's home in mind. Ambitious beginners as well as skilled workers will find complete guidance in the detailed building plans and photos of each piece.
by Franklin H. Gottshall

Building Early American Furniture
More than 50 projects for early American decor that can be shaped and built with tools almost everyone has around the home workshop. An emphasis on simplicity puts these beautiful reproductions within reach at minimal cost.
by Joseph Daniele

New Life for an Old House
What you can and can't do to revive, restore, renovate, and remodel a handyman special. In these pages are the answers for almost any question a used-home owner could ask.
by Grant Mallett

How to Build 35 Great Clocks
Complete with working plans, drawings, and instructions for building a variety of wooden clocks. The projects themselves offer a choice in building complexity, and all of them are of equally fine quality.
by Joseph Daniele

Custom Knifemaking
Ten different, increasingly difficult projects that together constitute a survey of knifemaking skills. Learn how to cut, shape, heat treat, and finish a knife.
by Tim McCreight

Woodcarving Illustrated
Easy-to-carve projects pictured in step-by-step diagrams, complete with detailed painting instructions. Ten explicit lessons on a range of projects, each with up to 50 illustrations.
by Roger Schroeder and Paul McCarthy

Woodcarving Illustrated Book 2
Eight useful projects you can make out of wood. Each is presented in a detailed, step-by-step format illustrated by up to 50 drawings. The finished piece is pictured in a full-page photo.
by Paul McCarthy and Roger Schroeder

Available at your local bookstore, or for complete ordering information, write:
Stackpole Books
Dept. CC
Cameron and Kelker Streets
Harrisburg, PA 17105
For fast service credit card users may call 1-800-READ-NOW
In Pennsylvania, call 717-234-5041